THE ARTISTS' COOKBOOK

THE ARTISTS' COOKBOOK

INTRODUCTION BY HENRY MOORE

PREFACE BY JOCELYN STEVENS

Macdonald Orbis

A _Macdonald Orbis_ BOOK

© In the work: Mobius International Limited/
Lion & Unicorn Press, London 1987
© Illustrations: Royal College of Art, London 1987

First published in Great Britain in 1987
by Macdonald & Co (Publishers) Ltd
London & Sydney

A member of BPCC plc

British Library Cataloguing in Publication Data

The Artists' Cookbook
    I. Cookery, International
    641.5   TX725.AI

    ISBN 0-356-13925-5

Filmset by Dorchester Typesetting Group Ltd

**Printed and bound in Spain by Graficromo,
S.A. — Córdoba**

Editor: Gilly Abrahams
Designer: Ingrid Mason
Creative Services: Mustafa Sami

Macdonald & Co (Publishers) Ltd
Greater London House
Hampstead Road
London NW1 7QX

CONTENTS

Introductions to books on recipes and food are usually written by those who have made their living from being gourmets. This introduction is certainly the exception. I have spent my life making sculptures, not sorbets – but all the time fuelled by thoughts, at least, of the meals my mother cooked in my native Yorkshire – fine English fare like mutton stew and rabbit pie. My wife Irina also prefers good, wholesome, English cooking. It is she who chooses the meat and fish we eat – and of course the large choice of garden-fresh vegetables.

During my life I have been lucky to have known two great cooks, my wife and my mother. I owe them my thanks for being well fed and looked after. As a result of this upbringing, I'm afraid I can't agree with the idea that, in order to be truly creative, an artist has to be underfed. I believe the varied and delightful offerings presented here by the staff and friends of the Royal College of Art more than prove my point.

Henry Moore

Having had more bad dinners in school and college dining halls than even I felt I deserved, when I came to the Royal College of Art, I had every reason to expect that artists and designers would be more preoccupied with cerebral pleasures. Imagine, therefore, my delight on my first day to find that I had arrived in an institution where the school dinner has been developed into an art form in its own right – where the chicken casserole consistently outshines its more elevated 'coq au vin' cousin and where the 'spotted dick' (which I have chosen as my recipe for this book) rivals any crème brûlée.

Now at last I know that the way to a man's art must surely be through his stomach.

Jocelyn Stevens

STARTERS

JESSICA WIDDEN

I cauliflower

Salt

A knob of butter

Nutmeg to taste

Pepper

Boil the cauliflower florets in 1-2 pints salted water for approximately 10 minutes. Remove the cauliflower from the pan and reserve the water. Blend or sieve the cauliflower. Put in saucepan with the butter, nutmeg, pepper and water and reheat.

Very good, especially if you are slimming – just leave out the butter and you have a lovely low-calorie soup.

ILLUSTRATION BY **DEREK MARTIN**

KRYSIA BROCHOCKA

ILLUSTRATION BY CHERRY DENMAN

I large head celery

I medium onion

I pint chicken stock

Salt and pepper

Small carton single cream

Chop the celery and onion and simmer in seasoned stock until soft. Place in blender and mix until smooth. Return to saucepan and add cream to taste.

WATERCRESS SOUP

JEAN SOUTHWOOD

ILLUSTRATION BY **KRISTIN JAKOB**

I lb floury potatoes
2 pints water
I leek, roughly chopped
I large bunch watercress, roughly chopped
Salt and black pepper
Whipped cream or yogurt

Cook the potatoes in about 2 pints of salted water (I find stock spoils the flavour of this delicate soup). When half-cooked, add the leek – then when nearly cooked add the watercress. Cook for a few minutes longer then pass the vegetables through a sieve or liquidizer. Use as much of the liquid as necessary to make your soup. Adjust the seasoning. Serve very hot with a spoonful of whipped cream or yogurt on the top and a small sprig of watercress.

I vary this recipe according to what I have in the garden or larder – sometimes I use a good handful of spinach together with about a handful of sorrel. Another alternative is lettuce. Any of these ingredients makes a delicious fresh soup.

ROSEMARY WILSON

ILLUSTRATION BY **JOANNA LEWIS**

Serves 4 – although the quantities are small, it is a rich soup.

2 very ripe avocados

1 pint chicken stock

Salt and pepper

Single cream

Chopped parsley

Chop the avocado flesh into the stock, then liquidize. Season with salt and pepper, then chill in the refrigerator.
    Serve topped with a spoonful of single cream and a sprinkling of chopped parsley.

ROBERT BUHLER

8 large oysters

8 rashers streaky bacon, rinds removed

Hot toast, buttered

Wrap each oyster in a bacon rasher. Fasten rolls with small skewers or wooden cocktail sticks. Grill for 4-6 minutes, or bake in the oven at 200°C / 400°F, gas mark 6, for 10 minutes. Place each roll on a slice of hot buttered toast.

Chicken livers or calves' liver

Butter

Salt

Cayenne pepper

8 large prunes, soaked or cooked

8 rashers streaky bacon, rind removed

8 slices of bread, fried in butter

A few stuffed olives

Cut liver into 8 pieces and fry in butter. Season with salt and a dusting of cayenne. Stone the prunes and stuff them with liver. Wrap each stuffed prune in a bacon rasher; secure with a wooden cocktail stick. Bake for 8 minutes in a hot oven.

To serve, put each 'devil' on a square of fried bread. Garnish with olives stuffed with pimento.

JEAN SOUTHWOOD

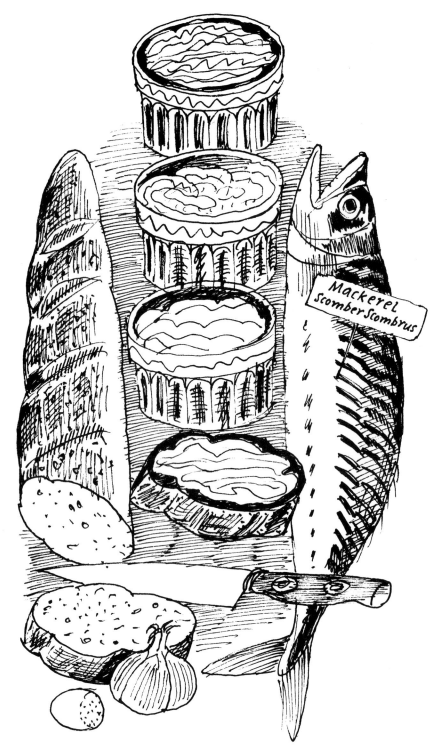

1 whole smoked mackerel

8 oz butter

Juice of 1 lemon

1 garlic clove, crushed

Salt and pepper

¼ nutmeg, grated

2 tablespoons double cream

Skin and flake the fish, pound with 6 oz of the butter and when fairly smooth, add the juice of 1 lemon and all the other ingredients. Taste and adjust seasoning.

Put into one or two small pâté dishes, cover with melted or clarified butter and place in refrigerator until ready for use.

Serve with lemon quarters, tartines (see below) and butter.

TARTINES
1 French loaf, cut in ¼-inch-thick slices and baked on an oiled tray in the oven until brown and crispy.

ILLUSTRATION BY **ROGER NICHOLSON**

DUNCAN OPPENHEIM

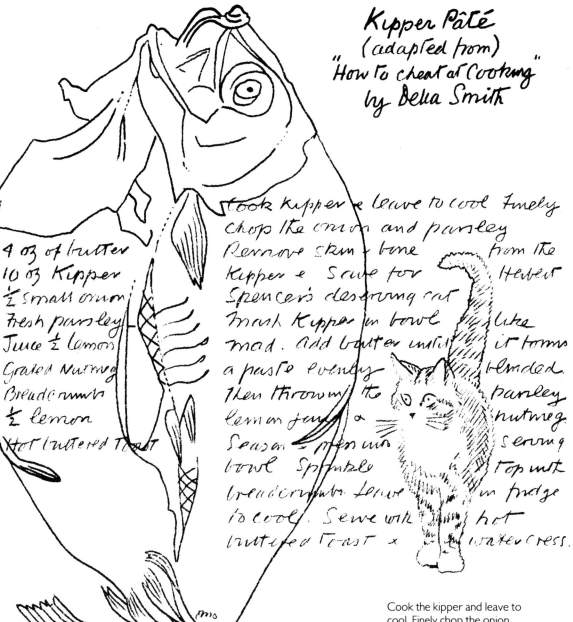

Kipper Pâté
(adapted from)
"How to cheat at Cooking"
by Delia Smith

4 oz of butter
10 oz Kipper
½ small onion
Fresh parsley
Juice ½ lemon
Grated Nutmeg
Breadcrumbs
½ lemon
Hot buttered Toast

Cook kipper & leave to cool. Finely chop the onion and parsley. Remove skin & bone from the Kipper & Save for Herbert Spencer's deserving cat. Mash Kipper in bowl like mad. Add butter until it forms a paste evenly blended. Then throw in the onion parsley lemon juice & nutmeg. Season & then into serving bowl. Sprinkle Top with breadcrumbs. Leave in fridge to cool. Serve with hot buttered Toast x watercress.

*Herbert Spencer is
ex-Professor of Graphics
at the Royal College of Art.

10 oz kipper
½ a small onion
Fresh parsley
4 oz butter
Juice of ½ lemon
Grated nutmeg
Black pepper
Breadcrumbs

Cook the kipper and leave to cool. Finely chop the onion and parsley. Remove skin and bones from the kipper and save for Herbert Spencer's deserving cat.*

Mash the kipper in a bowl. Add butter until the mixture forms an evenly blended paste, then throw in the onion, parsley, lemon juice and nutmeg. Season with pepper, then press into the serving bowl. Sprinkle breadcrumbs over the top and chill in fridge. Serve with hot buttered toast and watercress.

BERNARD MEADOWS

ILLUSTRATION BY **MICHAEL HEINDORFF**

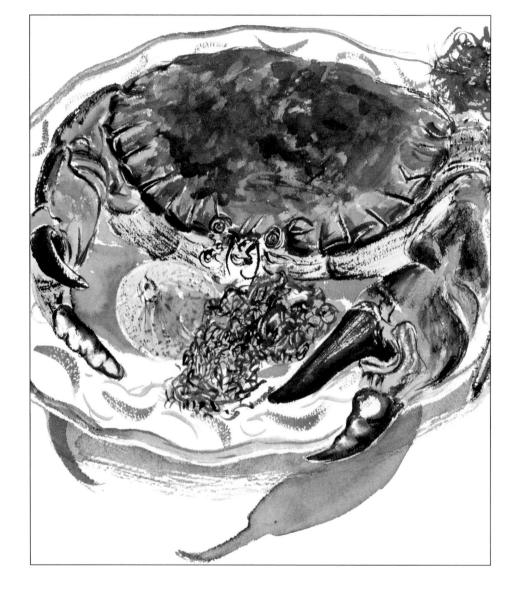

I oz butter	½ level teaspoon powdered saffron
I tablespoon olive oil	8 oz white fish, cut in pieces
I medium-sized onion, chopped	Salt and black pepper
2 carrots, chopped	I medium-sized cooked crab
I celery stick, chopped	Nutmeg
2 tomatoes, chopped	Cayenne pepper
I garlic clove, crushed	Chopped parsley
2 pints water	I glass dry vermouth or sherry
2 potatoes, diced	⅛ pint cream
Lemon peel	
A pinch of mixed herbs	

Melt the butter in a saucepan and add the olive oil, onion, carrot, celery, tomatoes and garlic. Cook over a low heat for 6-10 minutes, then add the water, diced potatoes, lemon peel, mixed herbs, saffron and white fish. Season with salt and black pepper and bring to the boil. Cook for about 20 minutes or until the vegetables are tender, then purée the mixture using a blender or sieve.

Transfer the purée to a pan, add the crabmeat and cook until really hot (about 5 minutes). Season with nutmeg and cayenne pepper and add chopped parsley and vermouth or sherry. Just before serving add the cream and reheat but do not boil.

MARGARET CALVERT

Eggs (2 or 3 per person)

Milk

Salt

Pepper

A knob of butter

Cream

Beat the eggs with a fork, adding a little milk, salt and pepper.

Melt the butter in a heavy saucepan over low heat. Pour in the eggs, stirring slowly and continuously until thick and creamy.

Remove from the heat and stir in a little cream to prevent the eggs from overcooking while still in the pan. This will also improve the flavour and give the eggs a light, creamy texture.

Serve immediately with hot buttered toast, some smoked salmon and a glass of Champagne.

DAVID QUEENSBERRY

Usually taramasalata is a gastronomic disaster as it is full of bread or some other padding and, mistakenly I feel, has garlic in it. For a successful paste, use the freshest smoked cod's roe you can find – and never use the kind sold in jars.

8 oz smoked cod's roe

2 oz good quality olive oil

Juice of ¼ lemon

Freshly ground black pepper

Remove the membrane from the roe and discard any pieces of roe that have gone hard or lumpy.

Put the roe in a bowl and add the oil slowly, mixing with a fork. (Never use a blender as it smashes the roe up into a horrible homogenized mixture.)

Squeeze in the lemon juice and a generous sprinkling of black pepper. You should end up with a viscous paste.

Put the paste into small containers such as egg cups or ramekins. Serve with hot toast and iced vodka. (Cod's roe does not go well with wine – it gives it the most evil taste.)

PHOTOGRAPH BY **JULIA HEDGECOE**

MARGARET CASSON

2 tins consommé

¼ pint single cream

2 oz Danish lumpfish 'caviar'

A few chives

Divide the consommé between six soup bowls and put in the fridge to set. When ready to use, pour sufficient cream on top just to cover the consommé and spoon the 'caviar' over the cream. Top with chopped chives.

RICHARD CAWLEY

4 oz prunes (those sold as 'no soak')

2 fluid oz port

5 oz Stilton, mashed with a fork

½ pint chicken or vegetable stock

1 sachet powdered gelatin

¼ pint double or whipping cream, whisked until thick and airy but not stiff

1 egg white (size 3), whisked with a pinch of salt until stiff but not dry

1 small red-skinned eating apple, cored and diced

4 small spring onions, trimmed and chopped (including green part)

Vinaigrette dressing, well spiked with dry English mustard

Place prunes in a small bowl, pour over port, cover tightly and leave to soak overnight.

Liquidize the cheese with half the stock, and dissolve the gelatin in the remaining stock according to the instructions on the packet. Pour both these mixtures into a medium-sized bowl, mix together and chill until just beginning to set.

Meanwhile, tip the prunes into a small saucepan and cook, tightly covered, over a very low heat for 10 minutes. By this time the prunes will be very soft and the liquid will have been absorbed. Allow to cool, then remove the stones and chop the flesh very finely, if possible in a food processor.

Fold first the cream and then the beaten egg white into the thickening cheese mixture.

Pour half this mixture into an oiled 1½-pint loaf tin and chill. When the mixture has set, cover with the chopped prunes, pressing them gently into the surface. Pour over the remainder of the cheese mixture and chill until set.

Mix the apple with the onion and toss in the dressing.

Dip the loaf tin briefly in hot water. Unmould terrine and cut into 1-inch slices. To serve, place a slice of the terrine in the centre of each plate and spoon a little of the salad around it.

BRIAN TATTERSFIELD

A savoury version (based on a recipe by Michael Smith) which can either be served as a first course, as it is in Yorkshire, or as an accompaniment to roast pork.

1 large onion, chopped

4 oz fresh white breadcrumbs

2 oz coarse oatmeal

2 level teaspoons chopped sage leaves, or 2 teaspoons dried sage

1 level teaspoon chopped fresh parsley

Salt

Freshly ground pepper

½ teaspoon grated orange or lemon rind

2 eggs, beaten

Pork drippings or 1 oz butter

Boil the chopped onion until tender in enough lightly salted water to cover. Strain, retaining the liquid, and leave to cool.

Mix together the rest of the ingredients, except the eggs and the fat, in a bowl. Add the onion and enough of the water to form a loose mixture. Stir in the beaten eggs. The mixture should be sloppy but not runny.

In a roasting tin or 2 smaller tins, heat some of the pork drippings or 1 oz butter, until smoking. Pour in the pudding mixture and bake at 200-220°C/400-425°F, gas mark 6-7, until crisp and cooked – about 25 minutes. Cut into squares and serve.

Brian Tattersfield '86

CHICKEN PÂTÉ MECHTHILD

MECHTHILD NAWIASKY

1 large onion, sliced

2 carrots, sliced

2 bay leaves

A large pinch of thyme and parsley

3 cloves

4 peppercorns

Sea salt, to taste

1 roasting chicken

Bacon

Butter

Pepper

Soy sauce

Tabasco

Celery salt

Bring a large saucepan of water to the boil, add the onion, carrots, bay leaves, thyme, parsley, cloves, peppercorns and a sprinkling of sea salt, and simmer for a few minutes. Add the chicken and simmer until cooked. Skim the stock. Remove the chicken from the saucepan and take all the meat off the bones. Return the bones to the stock for further boiling. Strain later.

Fry very small cubes of bacon with the chicken liver, chopped fine, in butter, with salt and pepper. Put all the meat and liver through a mincer, adding some of the stock just to moisten; add some soy sauce, a few drops of Tabasco and a dusting of celery salt. Taste and adjust if necessary. Put into a pâté dish. Refrigerate and serve when required.

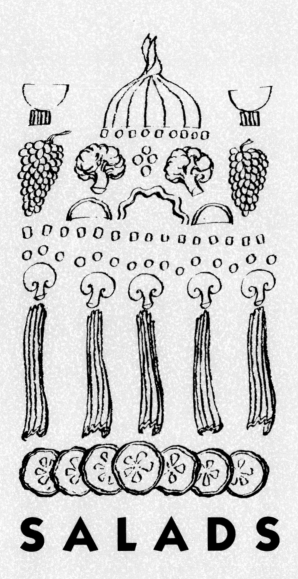

SALADS

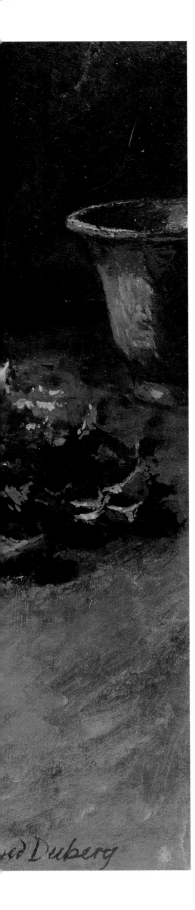

ud Dubery

FRED DUBERY

This is a winter salad made with curly endive and preferable to the floppy greenhouse-grown lettuces on sale in the dark months. Curly endive is by no means a modern exotic vegetable, for it was first brought to England in the sixteenth century; even so, it is sometimes difficult to find. It is like a round lettuce in size and shape, with curly leaves, dark green round the edges and pale green in the centre. The darker green parts tend to be slightly bitter, so if these are found to be disagreeable, they may be set aside and only the pale green leaves used in the salad. This dish is on the menu in many restaurants in Lyons and it is a great favourite.

| 1 curly endive |
| 2 eggs |
| 4 oz streaky bacon or roast belly of pork |
| 2 slices white bread, cut into ½-inch cubes |

FOR THE VINAIGRETTE:

| 1 teaspoon salt |
| ½ teaspoon freshly ground black pepper |
| 1 teaspoon French mustard |
| 1 shallot, finely chopped |
| 1 garlic clove, chopped |
| 1 dessertspoon finely chopped parsley |
| 2 tablespoons tarragon vinegar |
| Juice of ½ lemon |
| 6 tablespoons olive oil |

Prepare the vinaigrette by putting the salt and pepper into a bowl. Add the French mustard, shallot, garlic and parsley. Then add the vinegar and lemon juice and mix well. Finally, pour on the olive oil very slowly, beating all the time.

To prepare the salad, pull apart and wash the curly endive, separating the leaves according to taste. Remove the excess water, using a salad shaker. Hard boil the eggs, peel and set aside to cool before cutting into quarters. Cut the bacon into pieces about 1 inch long before frying; likewise, if you are using pieces of roast pork, cut these into small cubes and fry. While the fat is still hot, toss in the bread cubes and fry until brown.

Put the curly endive, eggs, meat and fried bread cubes into a bowl and mix well. Dress with a generous portion of the sauce vinaigrette just before serving.

MECHTHILD NAWIASKY

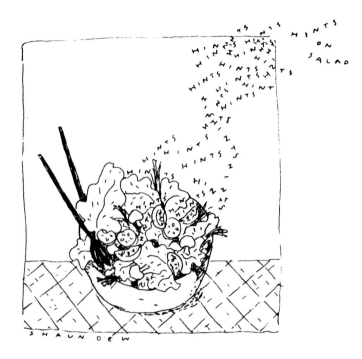

ILLUSTRATION BY **SHAUN DEW**

In my early days, vegetables for salads were not mixed up together – each was deemed to deserve its own dressing, even when on the table at the same time. I noticed the ostriches at the zoo, being served a mixture of vegetation, chopped up indiscriminately, looking disdainfully down at it, picking out a very few morsels and walking away. Many salads induce in me the same reaction. I shall now give a few hints on how to treat the admirable plants which serve us as salads.

1. Do not mix them up.
2. Bring out their individual flavour with a dressing especially invented for them and them alone.

LETTUCE
Mix a very little wine vinegar in which chopped tarragon leaves have marinated, with lemon juice (more than vinegar) tempered with a little sugar, a very little pressed garlic, some salt and freshly ground white pepper. Scrape half a Spanish onion, only the juice, not the flesh, and add to the lemon juice with a timid dusting of powdered English mustard, a trace of celery salt, a drop or two of Tabasco and a lot of premier-pressé olive oil. Taste for harmony and correct if necessary. Pour over salad and stir delicately.

AÏOLI
Serve this garlic mayonnaise with cooked, cold globe artichokes, grated celeriac or carrots when they are young and other cold vegetables. Put 1 or 2 egg yolks (without a trace of egg white) in a bowl and stir till smooth. Add, drop by drop, premier-pressé olive oil, till the mixture really thickens, then add the oil a little quicker. Add salt and freshly ground white pepper, lemon juice and a little sugar, very little vinegar and a lot of garlic squeezed through a garlic press. If you wish, you can also add the other ingredients which went into the lettuce dressing: celery salt and Tabasco. Left-over aïoli can go into a lettuce dressing, with moderation. Bitter salads do well with aïoli.

CUCUMBER
Peel, slice very thinly and let stand for an hour in a little salt and wine vinegar, then dust with freshly ground black pepper. Stir.

GREEN PEPPERS
Can be eaten without any dressing, or dipped in a little aïoli.

TOMATOES
Dip for a second into boiling water, one at a time so as not to cook them, peel off the skins and slice. Grate some onion juice over them, add a moderate sprinkling of wine vinegar and more of lemon juice mixed with a little sugar. Add some premier-pressé olive oil, not too much, some salt and freshly ground black pepper. Sprinkle some very finely chopped parsley over the salad and put it aside for an hour or so, to let flavours amalgamate. Stir.

BEETROOT
Cook and peel, slice finely, add caraway seeds, salt and freshly ground pepper, a little wine vinegar and lemon juice mixed with sugar (very little of that) and olive oil. Let it stand for a while. Stir. Never serve beetroot in the same dish with any other salads because it will make the others look as if they came from a battlefield. This also applies to tomatoes when ripe and properly peeled.

GILLIAN PATTERSON

ILLUSTRATION BY LOUISE BRIERLEY

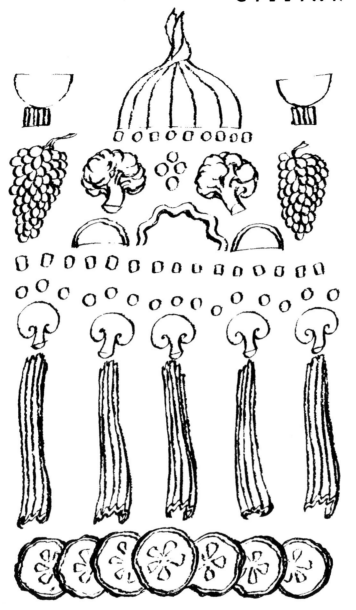

This salad arose from my dislike of lettuce. The amounts of ingredients depend on personal choice and availability.

Chicory

Green peppers

Raw baby mushrooms

Defrosted frozen peas

A tin of sweet corn

Celery

Green grapes

Young cauliflower florets

Cucumber

Spring onions

Chopped walnuts

Chop any of the ingredients needing it. Mix in a bowl, keeping aside a little of each ingredient to scatter on the top.

FOR THE DRESSING:

1 garlic clove (or use garlic salt)

2 teaspoons castor sugar

½ teaspoon salt

Black pepper

1 teaspoon dried mint

Olive oil

Vinegar

Crush the garlic and add the sugar, salt, pepper and mint. Mix the oil in slowly. Add the vinegar slowly, mixing vigorously so that the oil has no chance to form globules. The amount added is a matter of personal taste, so keep testing. The result should be slightly sweet; more sugar can be added if necessary. Leave to stand for a few minutes. Stir vigorously before pouring over the salad and tossing so that all the ingredients are well coated.

MICHAEL ROTHENSTEIN

I like salads, but it can get boring always having them jumbled up in a bowl. This one is made in layers, with peeled, sliced oranges at the bottom, covered with slices of avocado, then kiwi fruit – I don't actually like kiwi fruit all that much, but they look so amusing – topped with layers of Parma ham, raw carrots and, finally, gravlax (raw salmon pickled with dill).

You can make a salad like this in endless combinations, but the trick is to get a mixture of tastes and textures – salty, bland, soft, crunchy. At home we use smoked salmon, eel fillets, bresaola, Westphalian smoked ham or smoked mackerel fillets with vegetables such as fennel or string beans cooked for just a few minutes. Mozzarella cheese is a good bland foil to the sharper tastes. For fruit we use peaches, pears, nectarines but not apples – they go brown and spoil the look.

I don't put a dressing on the salad – just a few drops of olive or walnut oil and a squeeze of lemon on the vegetables.

RICHARD CAWLEY

This delicious and unusual salad course is a 'parade' of flavours both hot and cold, and makes an excellent starter or light lunch. Should you really wish to impress, change the name of this dish from 'Parade' to 'Cavalcade' by making four different fillings.

Fill some of the pasties with the two fillings given in this recipe, and the rest with either chilled garlic butter or finely chopped ham mixed with a little redcurrant jelly and a little mustard.

Serves 6

---

2 oz goats' cheese, or other soft cheese

1 spring onion, trimmed and finely chopped

Salt and freshly ground black pepper

Approximately 12 oz puff pastry, thawed if frozen

1 egg yolk, beaten with a little milk

12 smoked oysters, drained of oil

A selection of salad leaves (these should be as varied and interesting as possible), washed, dried and torn into pieces

6 artichoke bottoms (drained if tinned), thinly sliced across

Vinaigrette dressing, preferably made with walnut or hazelnut oil

Oil for deep frying

Mix the cheese with the onion and season well with salt and pepper.

Roll out the pastry very thinly and cut out 24 circles, approximately 2½ inches in diameter. Brush the edges of these with the egg yolk and milk glaze.

Place a smoked oyster in the centre of 12 of these pastry circles and divide the cheese mixture between the rest. Fold each pastry circle in half to enclose the filling, then pinch the edges firmly together to seal. Keep the two sorts of pasties separate. They can be prepared in advance up to this stage and kept for up to 12 hours in the fridge.

At the last minute toss the salad leaves and artichoke bottoms in the dressing and arrange them on six large plates.

Heat the oil and deep fry the little pasties, turning once, until puffed, crisp and golden. Drain on crumpled kitchen paper and keep warm, still keeping the two sorts separate.

To serve, arrange two of each kind of pasty on each plate, windmill fashion.

LILIAN DODD

ILLUSTRATION BY **CHARLES SHEARER**

3 hard-boiled eggs

2 tomatoes

1 large Spanish onion

1 sour cucumber

Salt and pepper

1 dessertspoon salad cream

1 dessertspoon vinegar

1 oz grated Cheddar cheese

Dice the eggs, tomatoes, onion and sour cucumber. Put into a bowl and add salt and pepper to taste. Add the salad cream and vinegar. Mix gently, trying not to break up the ingredients. Chill in fridge for several hours or overnight. Sprinkle the grated cheese on top just before serving.

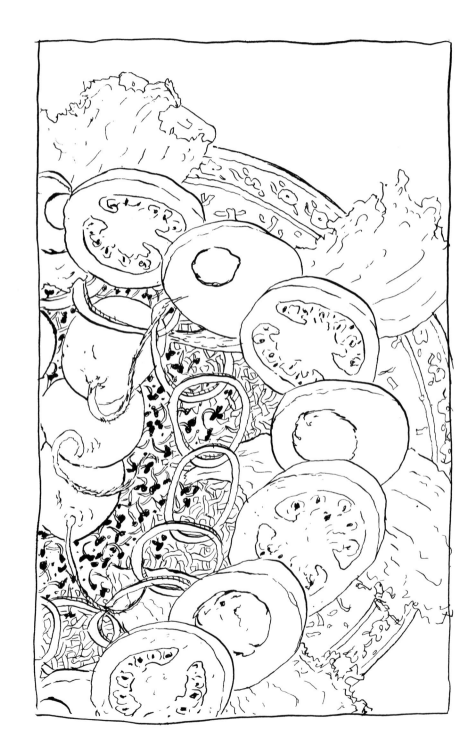

KRYSIA BROCHOCKA

I serve this dish with a bowl of crisp lettuce and a bowl of sliced tomatoes and courgettes sprinkled with sugar, lemon juice, vinegar and pepper. Baked potatoes are also nice with it.

ILLUSTRATION BY **VIRGINIA WILKINSON**

| 3 lb chicken |
| 8-12 oz dried apricots |
| 3 or 4 celery sticks |
| 1 medium pepper |
| 1 or 2 apples |
| Salted peanuts – as many or as few as liked |
| Raisins |

Cook the chicken, allow it to cool, then take the meat off the bones. Soak the apricots for 30 minutes. Chop the cooked chicken, the apricots, celery, pepper and apples and place in a bowl with the nuts and raisins.

FOR THE DRESSING:

| 10 fluid oz yogurt |
| 1-2 tablespoons single cream |
| Sugar |
| Lemon juice |
| Salt and pepper to taste |

Mix all the ingredients together until smooth and add to the salad. Mix well and allow to stand in fridge for an hour or so, or overnight if wished. Mix again before serving.

ILLUSTRATION BY **PAUL HOGARTH**

2 lb red cabbage

3 cooking apples

3 oz butter

1 small onion

A pinch of ground cloves

2 tablespoons wine vinegar

1 tablespoon sugar

Salt, to taste

10 fluid oz beef stock

A few tablespoons wine

Core and finely shred the cabbage and set aside.

Peel, core and thickly slice the apples, then fry them in the butter in a large saucepan.

Meanwhile, peel and roughly chop the onion. When the apples are lightly browned, add the cabbage, onion, cloves, vinegar, sugar and salt and stir well. Cook for a few minutes, stirring frequently, then add the stock.

Reduce the heat until the mixture is simmering gently, then cover with a lid and cook for about 45 minutes. Add the wine and cook for a further 15 minutes.

Serve warm or cold with cold ham.

PASTA, PIES AND PIZZA

POLENTA VITICUSO

EDUARDO PAOLOZZI

My father and mother emigrated to Scotland in the twenties and prepared their food as if they were still living in their village in the mountains of Frosinone.

Many dishes were made quickly, like eggs stirred into a bubbling pot of seasoned tomatoes or pimentos placed on top of a hot iron stove and eaten with oil and bread. Many peasant dishes, including this one, are eaten either hot or cold and for the hungry they are equally delicious.

Eduardo Paolozzi

Cooking polenta is like cooking pasta or rice. To a large pot of boiling salted water add two full handfuls of cornmeal. Stir continuously as if making porridge. When the mixture is thick, pour it into a large bowl, leaving room for a rich sauce of your choice. This is where the cook can be creative. My mother sometimes added spinach while the polenta was simmering. This looks beautiful.

Polenta can also be fried in slices with oil and garlic.

It is worth noting that variations of polenta are the national dish of Romania with rich butter and garlic sauces.

SPAGHETTI ALL'AGLIO (OR ALLE CIPOLLE OR AL BURRO)

Onions

Garlic

Olive oil

Spaghetti

Here is a dish I have cooked hundreds of times – it is known from one end of Italy to the other, from posh restaurants in Venice to humble villages in the hills of the Apennines. It is so good it can become addictive and yet it is dazzlingly simple.

Assuming you do not have much time and six special guests are coming in about two hours, put a large pot of salted water on to boil immediately. Meanwhile get on with chopping onions and some cloves of garlic and put these into a large frying pan with olive oil to simmer gently. Should you have some experience this might be done quickly, giving you time to wash and make a salad and lay out fruit and cheese.

By this time the water must be boiling. Put the spaghetti in and keep your eye on it. It must be cooked *al dente* (and not overdone). Experience again. Now cooked, the spaghetti should be drained – but leave a little water or it can be too dry. Add the cooked onions and garlic.

I have not overlooked the simpler version of this – no cooked sauce – just a little butter and a generous sprinkling of Parmesan cheese.

JOHN GOLDING

Pasta

1 large garlic clove, crushed

2 oz butter

1 tablespoon olive oil

2 bunches watercress, coarsely chopped

Grated Parmesan (optional)

Cook the pasta in the usual way, and while it is cooking prepare the sauce.

In a heavy frying pan lightly sauté the garlic in the butter and olive oil. When the garlic starts to colour, throw in the watercress, stalks and all. Stir until the watercress begins to melt but still retains some of its texture and colour. Pour over the cooked, drained pasta, toss and serve.

The traditional grated Parmesan is nice with this but not essential because of the sharp distinctive taste of the watercress. A fresh tomato salad makes a good accompaniment.

JULIAN TREVELYAN

I am very fond of all kinds of pasta. The following recipe is for a cold pasta, which can be eaten either as a starter or for a light lunch.

Serves 4

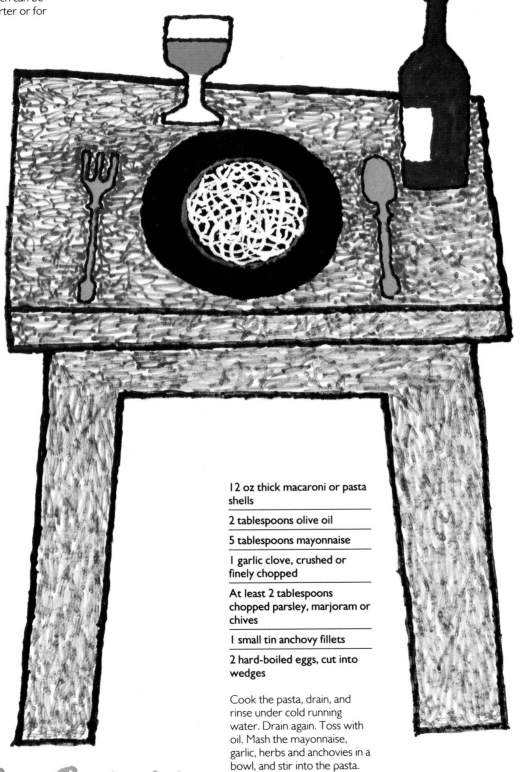

12 oz thick macaroni or pasta shells

2 tablespoons olive oil

5 tablespoons mayonnaise

1 garlic clove, crushed or finely chopped

At least 2 tablespoons chopped parsley, marjoram or chives

1 small tin anchovy fillets

2 hard-boiled eggs, cut into wedges

Cook the pasta, drain, and rinse under cold running water. Drain again. Toss with oil. Mash the mayonnaise, garlic, herbs and anchovies in a bowl, and stir into the pasta. Garnish with hard-boiled eggs and more parsley (or chives).

Julian Trevelyan '85

GIORGIO GIUGIARO

This sauce recipe is meant for the 'Marille' pasta I designed for Voiello. Unfortunately, it is rather difficult to buy 'Marillas' outside Italy, but macaroni would be a good substitute.

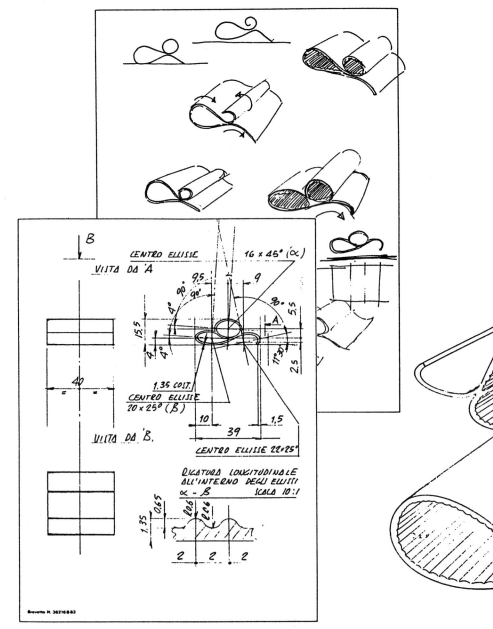

| 2 oz butter |
| 4 or 5 pieces of chilli |
| 2 tablespoons tomato purée |
| 2 fluid oz cream |
| 1 fluid oz vodka |
| 1 tablespoon cognac |
| 5 oz grated Parmesan cheese |
| 14 oz 'Marillas' or macaroni |
| 2 or 3 potatoes, thinly sliced (if you are using macaroni) |

Melt the butter in a frying pan, then add the chilli pieces.

In a bowl, mix the tomato purée with 4 tablespoons warm water. When well blended, pour it into the pan, together with the cream. Cook for 1 or 2 minutes, stirring constantly.

Remove the chilli pieces, and add the vodka and cognac. Let the sauce boil for 3 or 4 minutes, then add the Parmesan. Stir it well – 1 or 2 minutes are enough if you are a good mixer!

Meanwhile, cook the pasta in boiling water for about 15 minutes. (If you are using macaroni, add the sliced potatoes to the pan about 1 minute before the end of the cooking time.)

When the pasta is ready, drain, cover with the sauce, and . . . buon appetito!

Okonomiyaki – A Japanese Cabbage Pizza

ROGER NICHOLSON

Okonomi means something like 'to your taste' or 'your favourite flavouring', and Yaki means 'using fire or fire-grilled'.

Pronounced as it is spelt, it sounds like Economiyaki, which it truly is, and to my taste it is one of the best of all Japanese dishes. It consists of four parts:
A large proportion of finely chopped cabbage.
A binding of batter.
A savoury flavouring of meat, shrimp or squid.
A rich sauce.
There are endless variations of ingredients and flavourings so it is a dish which invites invention. It is a humble dish which is popular throughout Japan, but not one you can order in an expensive restaurant.

Serves 4

Make batter with 4 eggs, 2 cups flour, water.

Finely chop half a cabbage and 2 spring onions or small leeks. Mix together with the batter until it is ideal for making pancakes.

Fry finely sliced pork, or minced meat, or bacon or squid – separately or all together, as much or as little as desired.

Make a sauce of tomato ketchup and Worcester sauce mixed together.

Heat oil or butter in a large frying pan. Put in a good dollop of cabbage batter and press out to form a large pancake about ¾ inch thick. Place the savoury pieces on top and add another thin layer of cabbage. Turn when brown.

Divide into portions with a spatula and serve on hot plates. Add sauce. If available, sprinkle on Japanese seaweed and fish powder. In Kyoto and Osaka mayonnaise and mustard are also added.

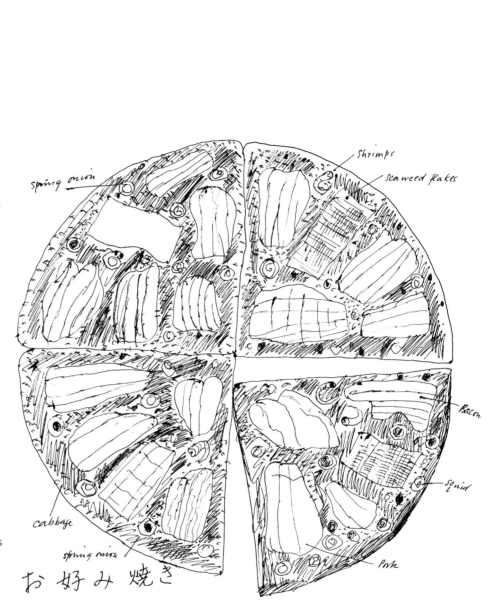

お好み焼き

41

NICHOLAS LAW

Serves 4

ILLUSTRATION BY **M O N I C A F I N E**

7 oz hard flour
2 eggs
1 well-washed leek
Milk
Minced beef
2 tomatoes
1 onion
1 pint yogurt, drained to ½ pint
Garlic (plenty)

Properly speaking this Afghan ravioli dish should be made with a flour and water paste, but it makes it rather heavy so a pasta dough (1 egg to 3½ oz flour) is preferable.

To make the dough, sift the flour on to a marble slab and make a well in the centre. Beat the eggs and pour into the well. Gradually incorporate the flour, using your fingertips until a smooth dough is formed. Shape it into a ball.

Roll the dough out as thinly as you can; cut circles not more than 2 inches in diameter and put very finely chopped raw leeks on half of them. Paint the edge with milk and press a matching circle on firmly as a lid. You cook these in rolling boiling water until *al dente*, drain them well and put into a hot dish.

Cover the discs with a good strong sauce made with beef, tomatoes and onion. Just before serving, top the dish with ice-cold strained yogurt spiked with plenty of chopped raw garlic. Serve at once, expecting to be surprised.

QUENTIN BLAKE

Smoked cod, haddock or whiting

Milk

Butter

Pasta

Pepper

Grated Parmesan (optional)

Take some smoked cod, haddock or whiting and put it in a pan with enough milk to partly cover it. Dot with pieces of butter, then simmer over a very low flame until the fish is cooked and flakes easily.

At the same time cook some pasta (if possible those shaped like shells) in boiling salted water until it is *al dente*. Drain the pasta.

Remove the fish from the milk; flake it and chop the skin. Boil the milk and butter to reduce to a sauce.

Add a sprinkling of pepper and mix everything together in a dish. With a bit of luck the pieces of fish will nestle felicitously in the pasta shells, though in fact they tend to sink to the bottom. You can also add grated Parmesan, but I don't like it. Serve with a sufficient quantity of Soave.

PHILLIP KING

PORTRAIT OF THE ARTIST AS A YOUNG MAN EATING SPAGHETTI

This is a very quick and tasty dish with a touch of distinction about it.

Serves 2

I lb broccoli
6-8 oz diced ham
8 oz carton cream cheese
Black pepper
Salt
¼ teaspoon paprika
I lb fresh pasta (wholewheat if preferred)

Steam the broccoli until just done – do not overcook. Remove from the pan and cut into 2-inch pieces, including stalks.

Place the ham in a frying pan without oil and brown over low heat. Add the broccoli and cheese, 5 twists of the pepper mill, a pinch of salt and the paprika.

Meanwhile, cook the pasta for 2-3 minutes (or longer if wholewheat) in rapidly boiling salted water. Drain pasta, place in bowl and pour sauce over it. Eat immediately.

JENY BENNETT

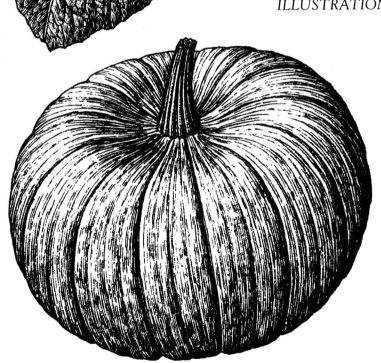

Make a pie crust using 1½ cups wholewheat flour, ⅓ cup sunflower oil, sesame seeds and water to bind. Cook at 180°C/350°F, gas mark 4, for 15 minutes before adding the filling.

ILLUSTRATION BY **KRISTIN JAKOB**

FILLING:
Chop the pumpkin flesh into large chunks and steam until tender. Purée with 2 tablespoons tahini, a pinch of nutmeg and salt to taste.

Pour the purée into the pie crust, decorate the top with chopped nuts and bake until golden brown on top (about 45 minutes).

BERNARD MYERS

This is a substantial meatless dish for 4-6 people. I have served it to 'mixed' parties of meat and non-meat eaters without the former being aware that they were eating a meatless meal. Although it is rather time consuming to prepare, the pancakes, aubergines, mushrooms and béchamel can be cooked in advance. The béchamel sauce must be heated very gently before assembling the pie; beat it perfectly smooth as it heats, and be careful not to burn it.

Other fillings can include thick tomato sauce, mozzarella cheese slices and Parmesan, with your favourite herbs.

FOR THE PANCAKES
(quantities given make 10 pancakes about 8 inches in diameter):

¾ pint cold milk and water (half and half)

4 eggs

A pinch of salt

8 oz sifted plain flour

2 oz melted butter

Oil or lard

Put the liquids, eggs and salt into a bowl, then add the flour and butter. Blend thoroughly by hand, or in a liquidizer for 1 minute. The batter should be perfectly smooth and just thick enough to coat the back of a spoon. Cover the batter and refrigerate for 2 hours if possible.

Cook the pancakes in a perfectly clean pan. Heat the pan dry. Use as little oil or lard as possible, just enough to coat the pan, and pour off any excess. As soon as the oil starts to smoke, pour in enough batter to thinly cover the pan and turn over as soon as the batter sets. The pancakes should be lightly freckled, thin and not too brown.

As the pancakes are cooked pile them up on greaseproof paper when still hot — interleave pancakes with paper. Keep the pile between two plates in a cool place.

FOR THE PIE:

2 large aubergines

Salt

12 oz mushrooms

Olive oil

2½ oz butter

2½ oz flour

1½ pints milk

Pepper

Grated nutmeg

Grated Cheddar cheese

Slice the aubergines ⅛ inch thick, sprinkle with salt and leave for 30 minutes to draw out the moisture.

Meanwhile, slice the mushrooms thinly, stalks and all. Fry them lightly in oil without browning them.

To make the béchamel, melt the butter in a small saucepan. Stir in the flour and then the milk to make a smooth creamy sauce. Add seasoning and flavour with nutmeg.

Now rinse the aubergines thoroughly and dry them with kitchen paper. Heat the oil in a pan and fry the aubergine slices lightly until just golden on both sides. Dry them on kitchen paper.

ASSEMBLING THE PIE:

Butter a deep ovenproof dish the same diameter as the pancakes. Fill with alternate layers of pancake, béchamel sauce and aubergines, pancake, béchamel and mushrooms. Season each layer. Repeat until the dish is full, and cover the whole lot with a thick layer of béchamel. Sprinkle with a generous layer of coarsely grated Cheddar cheese. Cook in a fairly hot oven (200°C/400°F, gas mark 6) until the pie is brown on top (30-40 minutes). Serve volcanic and red hot.

JOY LAW

ILLUSTRATION BY **SUE BALFRE**

I lb cooked spinach

8 oz ricotta cheese

3 tablespoons Parmesan cheese

Salt and pepper

I lb shortcrust pastry

4 eggs plus I extra yolk

A little milk

Chop the spinach coarsely and leave to cool. Mix in the ricotta and Parmesan cheeses. Season well.

Line a deep cake tin with shortcrust pastry (setting aside enough for the lid) and fill to within an inch of the top with the spinach mixture. Make four deep wells in the mixture and break an egg into each. Put the pastry lid on, sealing it well with milk and glazing it with egg yolk, and marking it to tell you where the eggs are. Bake in a hot oven (200°C / 400°F, gas mark 6) for 40 minutes.

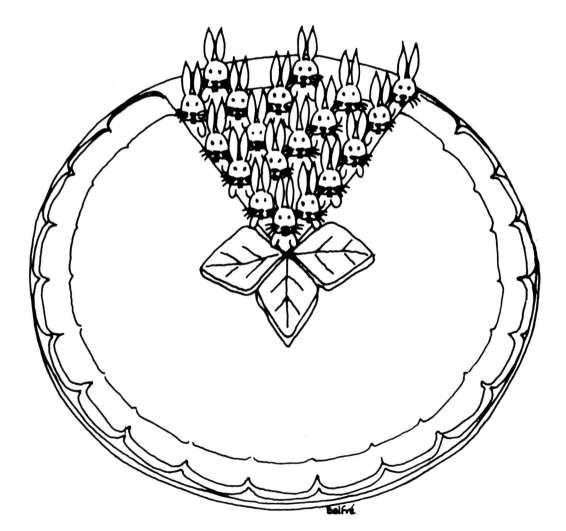

JANE GIBSON

ILLUSTRATION BY **PETER BROOKES**

BODY:

8 oz flour

4 oz fat

A pinch of salt

H_2O

FILLING:

1 lb sausage meat

2 apples

1 onion

A handful of fresh sage

Salt and pepper

GLAZE:

1 egg

TECHNIQUE

Prepare the body by mixing together flour, fat and salt. Add H_2O and wedge until required plasticity is obtained.

Roll out a slab and press-mould into a pie dish, reserving a slab for the lid.

Press the sausage meat into the base of the mould and cover with a layer of peeled, sliced apple. Add grated raw onion, chopped sage and salt and pepper.

Place the lid on top and join the edges neatly with a modelling tool. Glaze the lid with beaten egg.

Put in pre-heated kiln (190°C/375°F, gas mark 5) and fire for 40 minutes.

Can be eaten hot or cold.

6 oz pasta letters (illiterates may use spaghetti)

6 oz meat balls

4 fluid oz tomato sauce

I chopped onion

I tablespoon olive oil

3 tablespoons grated Parmesan cheese

Piecrust pastry

2 tablespoons milk

Boil the pasta letters in salted water until half-cooked, drain well, and leave to cool.

Chop the meat balls coarsely, mix with the pasta letters, and add the tomato sauce. Sauté the onion in oil until brown. Add mixture and heat for 5 minutes, then sprinkle with grated cheese.

Line a pie dish with pastry and pour in the mixture. Cover with the remaining pastry, pinch edges together, and prick all over to allow steam to escape. Brush with milk.

Bake at 220°C/425°F, gas mark 7, for about 20 minutes or until brown. May be served with a composing stick but this is not essential.

or
How to raid your fridge late on Boxing Day and be amply rewarded.

Making two pies at a time saves effort and they should keep for at least a week in the fridge.

Skin and bone a brace of pheasants. Open a bottle of wine now – one's patience is tried by the time you reach the third or fourth stringy leg. Cut any large pieces you still have into smaller pieces and fling the whole lot into a frying pan just sizzling with melted butter. Add a further 8 oz of similarly chopped veal fillet or chicken and a few rashers of bacon, also finely chopped. Season lightly.

When the pieces are browned, add a glass of red wine and reduce over a moderately high heat until virtually no liquid remains. Add sufficient chicken stock to cover the contents of the pan, then simmer for a few minutes. Set aside and then separate the meat from the stock.

Line two well-greased 1 lb rectangular loaf tins with a ¼-inch layer of shortcrust pastry made with 12 oz lard, 1½ lb flour, and a hefty pinch of salt. The pastry should come over the side of the tin by at least an inch all round, and it should be carefully persuaded to form an even layer at the corners.

Cram the meat in as neatly as possible and fill any gaps that are left with some of the stock, but do not overfill. Put on the pastry lid and carefully fold over the joined edges away from the sides of the tin. Coat with egg white and bake low down in a moderate oven for at least 1½ hours, covered with greaseproof paper for the first hour.

Allow the pie to cool in the tin, then make a small hole in the top of the crust. Add sufficient of the stock – with gelatin added – to fill the pie. Repeat every few hours until no more stock is absorbed. Remove the pies from the tins before storing in the fridge.

Serve cold and thinly sliced. Best accompanied by a tomato in the other pocket.

ILLUSTRATION BY **JOHN BRADLEY**

JOHN AND JULIA HEDGECOE

Serves 4

PHOTOGRAPH BY **JOHN HEDGECOE**

4 slices stale granary bread

Grated rind and juice of a small lemon

2 tablespoons finely chopped fennel leaves

10-12 fennel seeds, chopped

Salt

Freshly ground black pepper

Butter

4 mackerel or herring, boned but left whole

Make the bread into crumbs. Add lemon rind, fennel leaves and seeds, salt and pepper to taste. Mix thoroughly.

Melt some butter in a grill pan. Coat the skins of the fish in this. Turn the fish over, so that they are skin-side up, and put under a hot grill for 3-5 minutes. Remove. Turn the fish over and cover with the breadcrumb mixture; pack more into the centre between the flesh. Baste with melted butter and dot with more butter. Cook under a medium grill until done and the top is just crisp.

Squeeze some lemon juice over the fish and serve with the juices from the pan. Plain boiled potatoes or fresh bread go well with this dish, followed by a crisp winter or summer salad.

FISH MOUSSE FOR EIGHT

JOY LAW

ILLUSTRATION BY EMMA CHICHESTER-CLARKE

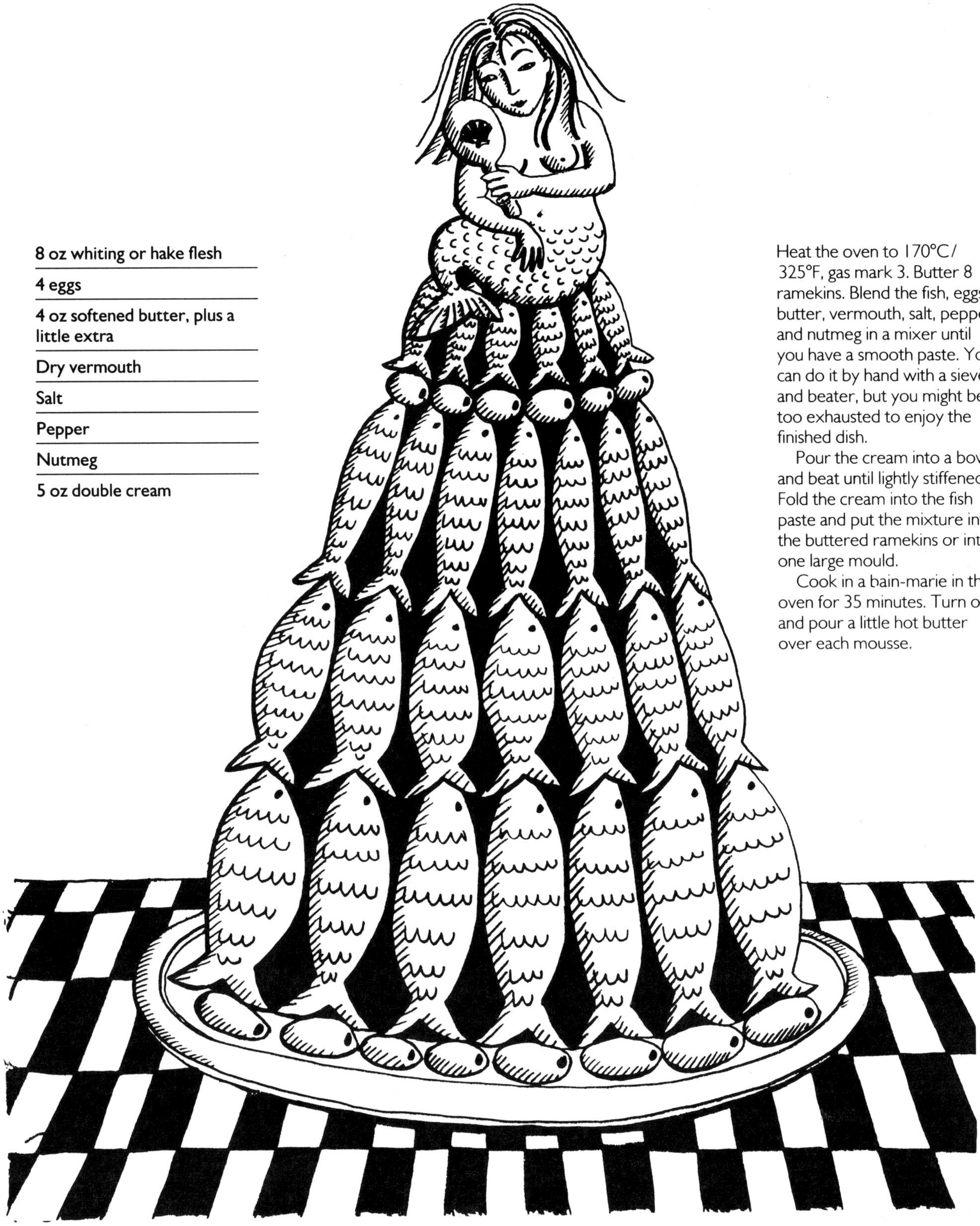

8 oz whiting or hake flesh
4 eggs
4 oz softened butter, plus a little extra
Dry vermouth
Salt
Pepper
Nutmeg
5 oz double cream

Heat the oven to 170°C/325°F, gas mark 3. Butter 8 ramekins. Blend the fish, eggs, butter, vermouth, salt, pepper and nutmeg in a mixer until you have a smooth paste. You can do it by hand with a sieve and beater, but you might be too exhausted to enjoy the finished dish.

Pour the cream into a bowl and beat until lightly stiffened. Fold the cream into the fish paste and put the mixture into the buttered ramekins or into one large mould.

Cook in a bain-marie in the oven for 35 minutes. Turn out and pour a little hot butter over each mousse.

SPICY MACKEREL

BOBBY GILL

Mackerel

Onions

Cloves

Bay leaf

Peppercorns

Parsley

A pinch of thyme

A pinch of mace

A pinch of salt

Malt vinegar

Clean and wash the fish, then cut off the heads and fins. Lay the fish in a baking dish with sliced onions, spices, herbs and salt. Cover with vinegar and bake in a moderate oven until thoroughly cooked – about 30-40 minutes.

Lift out fish and place in a deep serving dish. Strain the vinegar over the fish. Serve when cold, with salad.

ALF DUNN

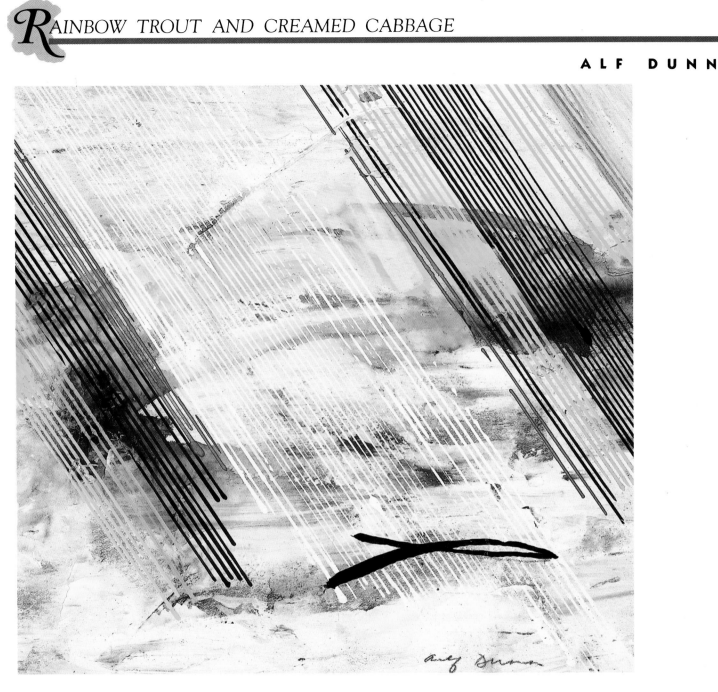

2 medium-sized trout	
Garlic	
Lemon juice	
2 oz flaked almonds	
Butter	
2 oz button mushrooms, finely sliced	
Salt and pepper	
8 oz white cabbage, finely sliced	
2 fluid oz single cream	
Slices of lemon	

Wash and clean the trout, leaving the heads on. Wipe the inside of the fish with half a clove of garlic and sprinkle with lemon juice. Toast the flaked almonds in ½ oz butter and when they begin to turn brown add the mushrooms. Cook briskly for a few minutes, then spoon inside the trout. Slit the skin along the backbone of the trout and place the fish on oiled kitchen foil on the grill pan. Wipe the fish with a smear of butter and sprinkle with salt and black pepper. Grill under a medium heat for approximately 10 minutes; turn the fish and repeat.

While the fish is cooking, heat 1 oz butter in a frying pan over a gentle heat and add the finely sliced garlic, a sprinkling of salt and black pepper. Increase the heat and add the sliced cabbage. Cook for approximately 10 minutes, stirring occasionally, until the cabbage is golden but still crisp. Reduce the heat and stir in the cream, stirring gently until the cream is warm but not boiling.

Place the trout on a serving dish, surround with the cabbage and garnish with slices of lemon.

ROSEMARY WILSON

ILLUSTRATION BY CHRISTINE SIMPSON

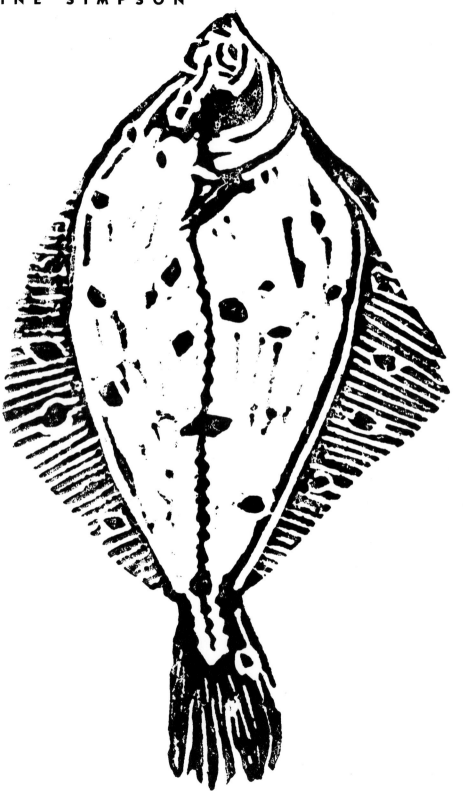

Serves 4

4 plaice fillets

¼ pint single cream

2 Gervais cheeses

A few chives

4 oz fresh shrimps (could be tinned or frozen)

Put plaice fillets into dish. Mix cream with cheese to form a thick mixture. Spread over fish. Chop chives. Peel shrimps. Cover fish with greaseproof paper to keep moist and place on middle shelf of oven. Cook at 170°C/ 325°F, gas mark 3, for 10 minutes. Turn up to 190°C/ 375°F, gas mark 5, and cook for another 10 minutes. Remove greaseproof paper. Sprinkle top with shrimps and chives. Leave in oven for 3-5 minutes, then serve with potatoes and salad.

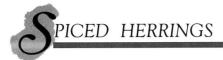

JOANNE BROGDEN

6 herrings, plump and fresh

1 dessertspoon brown sugar

2 large onions

4 bay leaves

6 cloves

6 coriander seeds, or more to taste

12 black peppercorns, crushed

¾ pint cider vinegar

Cut the heads off the herrings, just behind the hard side-gill, in front of the fin. You should be able simultaneously to pull away some gut. Slit through from anus to throat, completing the gutting. Leave any roes inside.

Rinse the fish under cold running water. Pack the fish flat into a shallow fireproof dish or casserole and sprinkle with the sugar. Peel the onions, slice them thinly and separate into rings. Sprinkle them over the fish decoratively. Add the other herbs and spices and the coarsely crushed peppercorns. Then pour the warmed cider vinegar over the whole lot.

Cover the dish with its lid or with foil and bake in a slow oven (150-170°C / 300-325°F, gas mark 2 or 3) for 1½ hours minimum. The longer the cooking, the better the flavour and the softer the bones.

JOANNE BROGDEN

This is a delicious and decorative dish for those who love shellfish and Normandy. The one is a fond reminder of the other.

Mussels are plump and ready for eating from October to March. When cooked, mussels have a beautiful melon colour ready to be enhanced by the fresh green parsley.

Serves 4

8 oz prawns
4 pints mussels
3 shallots or small onions
2 lb potatoes
A good knob of butter
Milk
1 large glass of Muscadet wine
2 bay leaves or bouquet garni
4-6 oz button mushrooms
A small sprig of French or English parsley, chopped

FOR THE SAUCE:

1 ½ oz butter
1 ½ oz flour
¾ pint prawn fumet and mussel liquid (see recipe)
3 tablespoons double cream

Shell the prawns and take off their heads, then gently stew the shells in ½ pint water, with the lid on the pan, to make a 'fumet'. Put the flesh on one side to be used later.

Meanwhile, wash the mussels in cool water and clean them with a small-bladed kitchen knife. Flick off any small barnacles and pull away, with a seesaw jerk, the weedy 'beard'. Discard any broken or cracked mussels and those which will not close when sharply tapped with your knife. Put each shining black beauty into a bowl of fresh water.

Peel and slice the shallots. Peel, boil and cream the potatoes with butter and a little milk. Keep warm until needed.

Using a good-sized saucepan, soften the sliced shallots in the butter over a low heat and with the lid on. When soft, stir in the wine, add the bay leaf or bouquet garni, then add the drained mussels to steam open and cook. Replace the lid, but keep looking to check progress. As the mussels open they release their juices into the liquid. Stir them about with a wooden spoon, to facilitate even cooking. If your saucepan is not large enough, cook the mussels in separate batches. Allow 3 minutes' cooking time after the mussels have opened.

Lift the cooked molluscs out of the pan and place in a bowl. Using one pair of shells still linked together as pincers, remove the mussel flesh and place on a dish. Discard the shells and any mussels which refuse to open. Add some of the cooking liquid to the fumet, to make it up to ¾ pint.

Now make the sauce. Melt the butter and add the flour to make a roux which you must cook gently for a few minutes. Remove from the heat and, stirring constantly, add the prawnshell and mussel liquid little by little. To achieve a thickened sauce, return the pan to the heat, stirring constantly, while reducing the liquid. Lastly add the cream.

Throw in the mussels and prawns to reheat, together with the sliced button mushrooms. Do not overcook.

Have ready a warmed serving dish and pipe the warm creamed potato all round the edge, making a low wall. Spoon the mussels, prawns and mushrooms on to the dish, inside the potato 'wall'. Individual scallop or porcelain shells may be similarly used. Add parsley as a final touch. Serve with a dry white wine.

NB: the cooked mussels in the sauce can be put in a secure lidded plastic container and kept in the deep freeze until needed.

DAN FERN

Serves 2-4

1 lb large shrimps or prawns

2 tablespoons cornflour

3 tablespoons wine vinegar

Salt

2 tablespoons soy sauce

5 teaspoons sugar

4 garlic cloves, crushed

1 ½ tablespoons finely chopped root ginger

1 ½ cups oil

4 oz cashew nuts

2 tablespoons chopped white of spring onions

Shell, rinse and pat dry shrimps. Lightly coat them in the cornflour and set aside in a bowl. Combine wine vinegar, salt, soy sauce and sugar in a bowl and set aside. In another bowl place the crushed garlic and ginger. Set aside.

Heat the oil in a wok and add the cashews. Cook until brown, remove and set aside. Add the shrimps, stir-fry quickly for about 2 minutes and remove with a perforated spoon.

Discard all but 2 tablespoons of the oil. Add the ginger, garlic and spring onion, stir-fry quickly and then add the vinegar mixture. When this boils, add the shrimps. When the shrimps are well coated, remove and mix in the cashews. Serve very hot with fried rice.

This dish was often served to visitors to the Isle of Wight in the nineteenth century. It was accompanied by thin slices of brown bread and butter, watercress and English sauce (hollandaise) and never by chips or any form of potatoes. . . .

ILLUSTRATION BY C A R E L W E I G H T

4 small whiting or flounders	
8 small herring	
4 very small mackerel	
1 pint coating batter	
4 oz cooked shelled prawns or the flesh of ½ shelled lobster	
Oil	
1 lemon, cut in 8 thin slices	

Clean the fish and remove the heads and tails. Pour the well-mixed batter into a shallow dish and lay all the fish in it, turning and rolling them gently until they are thinly coated all over. Do the same with the prawns or lobster, but keep them separate.

The fish can be deep or shallow fried as preferred, but oil must be used as butter does not give sufficient crispness. Put the fish in the oil only when it is really hot (about 200°C/400°F) and fry them very crisp and brown. Add the prawns or lobster at one side of the pan and fry for 2 or 3 minutes only. Longer cooking makes them tough.

Lift all the fish and shellfish on to a warmed flat dish and serve at once, garnished with slices of lemon.

ROBERT GOODDEN

Variation on a recipe by Christopher Muir.

Serves 4

ILLUSTRATION BY GILL BRADLEY

| 1 large green pepper |
| 1 lb tomatoes |
| 1 lb mushrooms |
| 1 packet Marks & Spencer's lobster soupmix |
| 8 fluid oz single cream |
| 8 oz cooked and peeled prawns |
| 2½ cups water |
| ½ teaspoon salt |
| 1 cup American long grain rice |
| 3 oz butter |

Slice and lightly fry the pepper, tomatoes and mushrooms. Blend the soupmix and some of the cream to a paste, stir in the rest of the cream and heat the mixture till it steams but does not boil, stirring continuously. Stir in the fried vegetables and simmer for 20 minutes, stirring occasionally. Remove from the heat, stir in the prawns and leave to cool.

While the mixture is simmering, bring the salted water to the boil, stir in the rice, cover and simmer for 20 minutes (until the rice is *al dente*). Stir occasionally. Remove from the heat and leave to stand for 5 minutes, or until all water has been absorbed. Turn into a deep dish, cover the rice with dollops of butter and place in a cool oven until the butter has percolated through the rice. Set aside to cool and serve cold with the prawns.

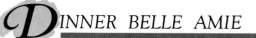

JOHN BELLANY

Serves 6

6 pints fresh mussels

2 oz butter

4 shallots, chopped

A few parsley sprigs

1 sprig thyme

1 bay leaf

Freshly ground black pepper

½ pint white wine

1 tablespoon flour

Scrub the mussels well, then drain in a colander. Melt half the butter in a large pan and gently fry the shallots until they are soft but not coloured. Add the herbs, pepper and wine, and then the mussels. Cover the pan and cook quickly, shaking the pan constantly, until the mussels open – this takes about 5 minutes. Discard any that remain closed.

Lift the mussels out of the pan using a draining spoon, and discard the empty half of each shell. Place the mussels in a heated serving dish and keep warm.

Boil the cooking liquor rapidly until it is reduced by about half, then strain into a clean pan. In a small bowl, blend the remainder of the butter with the flour to a smooth paste. Drop this into the simmering stock, a teaspoon at a time, and cook, stirring constantly, until the stock is smooth and has thickened. Pour over the mussels and sprinkle with chopped parsley.

2 medium-sized lobsters, about 2½ lb each

A few drops of olive oil

2 shallots, finely chopped

A few sprigs of parsley

1 sprig of tarragon

A few sprigs of chervil

½ pint white wine

1½ oz butter

1 oz flour

½ pint milk

2 teaspoons French mustard

4 tablespoons double cream

Pepper

10 oz grated Parmesan cheese

Split the lobsters in half, remove the black intestinal vein and discard together with the stomach. Take the flesh out of the shells and put on one side, together with the meat from the claws. Reserve the lobster shells and polish them with olive oil.

Put the shallots, parsley, tarragon and chervil into a saucepan with the wine. Cook, uncovered, over a moderate heat until the wine is reduced to about 4 tablespoons.

Melt the butter in another pan, stir in the flour and cook for about 1 minute. Gradually stir in the milk and bring to the boil, stirring all the time. Turn down the heat and stir in the mustard, the strained wine and the cream. Finally, stir in the lobster flesh, heat gently and season with pepper to taste. Spoon the lobster back into the shells and sprinkle with cheese. Put under a hot grill and cook for a couple of minutes.

Sweet flan pastry

2 lb Golden Delicious apples

Juice of 1 lemon

3 oz sugar

Chill the pastry for at least 30 minutes. Peel, halve and core the apples, then rub them with lemon juice.

Preheat oven to 190°C/375°F, gas mark 5.

In a heavy saucepan, gently heat the sugar with 2 tablespoons water until the syrup is a rich brown colour. Remove from the heat and let the bubbles subside, then pour the caramel into an ovenproof dish, turning it so that the bottom is evenly coated. Lay the apple halves upright and in overlapping circles on the caramel. Bake uncovered on the bottom shelf of the oven for 20 minutes, then cool slightly, allowing the steam to evaporate.

Roll out the chilled pastry dough to fit the top of the ovenproof dish and chill on a baking sheet for 15 minutes or until firm. Place the pastry circle over the apples to cover them completely. Prick the dough several times with a fork. Bake for 20 minutes or until the crust is light golden, then remove from the oven. When the pie is lukewarm, place a warmed serving dish over the top and invert. Remove the ovenproof dish and serve at once.

Invite 5 guests and insist they wear their best hats.

1½ pints live mussels

White wine

1 large sole, filleted and skinned and cut into strips

Court-bouillon

8 oz sea bass, halibut or monkfish, cut into strips

4 oz mushrooms

Butter

Salt and pepper

Lemon juice

A 9-inch circular vol-au-vent case, plus lid, made with 1 lb puff pastry

1 cooked lobster, diced into generous pieces

8 oz cooked shelled prawns

1 red pepper, grilled, skinned and cut into strips

3 egg yolks

¼ pint double cream

A dash of Pernod

Parsley

FOR THE VELOUTÉ SAUCE:

1 oz butter

2 tablespoons flour

1 pint fish stock, made with bones and fish trimmings

Steam open mussels in white wine; strain off liquid and reserve. Poach sole strips in court-bouillon. Poach bass, halibut or monkfish in court-bouillon. Cook mushrooms in butter with salt, pepper and lemon juice; remove from heat and reserve.

Make a velouté sauce with the butter, flour and stock; add mussel and mushroom liquids; simmer for 40 minutes; skim.

Warm the vol-au-vent case. Heat up seafood and vegetables in the velouté sauce. Mix the egg yolks with the juice of 1 lemon and the cream and add to stew; heat gently. Add a dash of Pernod, adjust seasoning and spoon into the warm pastry case.

Replace pastry lid, and garnish with parsley.

COQUILLES ET POIREAUX À LA MORNAY GRATINÉS

ANNE TYRRELL

Serves 2

8 leeks
8 scallops
½ pint dry white wine
½ bay leaf
Chopped spring onions
Salt and pepper
1 oz butter
1 oz flour
Single cream
Coarsely grated Swiss cheese
Finely grated Parmesan

Clean leeks thoroughly and chop into rounds. Cook in rapidly boiling salted water until tender, but still crunchy and green. Strain and divide between two gratin dishes.

Clean the scallops. Put the white wine, bay leaf, chopped spring onions, salt and pepper in a pan and simmer for 5 minutes, then add the scallops. Cover and simmer gently for 5 minutes. Remove scallops and place on the leeks. Strain the white wine mixture and set aside.

Make a basic roux with melted butter and flour. Add a little cream, stirring continuously until sauce thickens. Also add some of the strained white wine mixture. Flavour with salt and pepper; add grated cheese. Pour cheese sauce over scallops and leeks and sprinkle a little grated Parmesan cheese on top of each gratin dish. Place in a hot oven for a few minutes, then brown under a hot grill.

QUENTIN BLAKE

Kettlemar is an English name for the angler fish or monkfish. Probably no one uses the name any more, but the fish itself is popular and you can see this version of it on menus as monkfish kebabs or *lotte en brochette*. Angler fish is also the *coda di rospo* that you can sometimes see literally translated on Venetian menus as *tail of toad*. It has the reputation of appearing in disguise when scampi or lobster are not available; but it is very good in its own right.

Cut the flesh away from the cartilaginous backbone. This is easy to do as there are no other bones, and gives you two substantial strips of fish which you cut into suitable-sized pieces to go on the skewers. Alternate the pieces of fish with mushrooms, squares of bread dipped in olive oil, and folded pieces of streaky bacon. Ten or 15 minutes under the grill is sufficient to cook the fish and crisp the bread and the bacon. The firm flesh of the angler fish is very suitable for cooking on skewers; scallops are very good cooked this way too.

Skewers of Kettlemar

CHICKEN
AND
GAME

AZIZ R. KHAN

2 small chickens, jointed

FOR THE MARINADE:

1 small carton yogurt

1 large lemon, squeezed

2 level teaspoons salt

4 tablespoons oil

4 level tablespoons Tandoori spice (this is sold in tins)

Cut deep slashes into the chicken flesh with a sharp knife. Mix together all the marinade ingredients and pour over the chicken, making sure all the joints are well coated. Cover and leave in the fridge overnight.

Grill the chicken pieces for 15 minutes on each side under a moderate heat until the meat is cooked.

Serve the chicken with lettuce, sliced tomatoes and sliced onions or spring onions.

ILLUSTRATION BY **SUE HILTON**

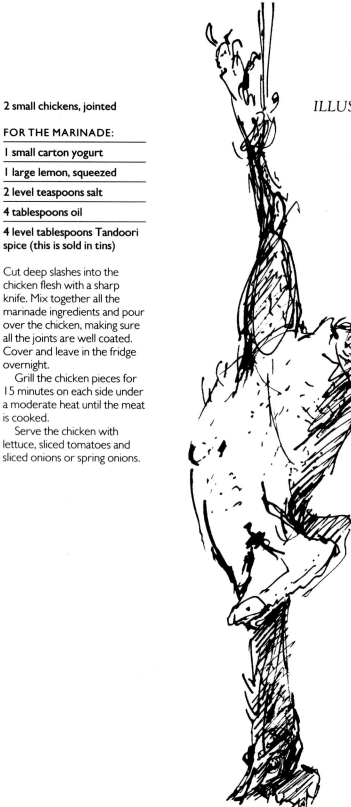

Serves 4

CASSEROLE:

4 chicken pieces

1 large packet frozen mixed vegetables, including sweetcorn

1 garlic clove (optional)

Salt and pepper

1 tin condensed chicken soup

Put chicken joints in casserole; arrange vegetables round chicken. Crush garlic with a pinch of salt and use to flavour soup; add extra salt and pepper as necessary. Pour seasoned soup over chicken mixture. Cover casserole with lid or kitchen foil and cook on centre shelf in moderately hot oven (190°C/375°F, gas mark 5) for 1½ hours. Remove foil about 30 minutes before end of cooking time.

ILLUSTRATION BY **ANDREW DAVIDSON**

POTATOES:

1½ lb potatoes

Salt and pepper

1 small onion

½ pint milk

½ oz butter or margarine

1 oz finely grated cheese

Peel and slice potatoes thinly and arrange in a greased shallow fireproof dish. Sprinkle with salt and pepper. Cover with finely chopped onion, then pour on milk. Dot with butter or margarine and sprinkle with cheese. Cover with kitchen foil and cook on the same shelf at same time as the chicken casserole, removing foil 15 minutes before the end of the cooking time.

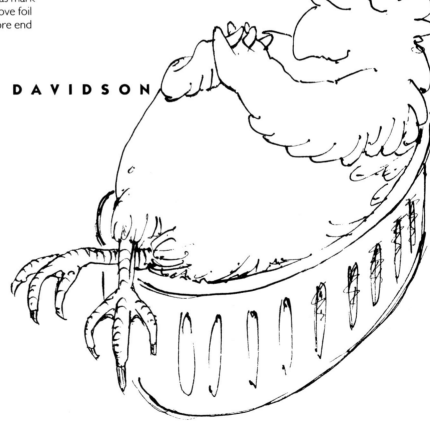

DOMINIC DE GRUNNE

(A Flemish dish which has nothing to do with Waterloo.)

ILLUSTRATION BY HANNAH FIRMIN

Onions

Leeks

Celery

Butter

Chicken or guinea fowl

Beef (or veal) stock

Seasoning to taste

Bay leaf and thyme or bouquet garni

2 or 3 egg yolks

Fresh cream

Slice the onions, leeks and celery. Fry them gently in butter in a heatproof casserole for 10 minutes.

Brown the chicken or guinea fowl on all sides. Pour some beef (or veal) stock over the vegetables; add seasoning, plus bay leaf and thyme (or bouquet garni). Settle the bird(s) to roost comfortably on the bed of vegetables. Cover and leave to cook on a low flame for 30-40 minutes depending on the size of the bird(s). Turn the bird(s) over once or twice.

In the meantime, beat the egg yolks and mix them very thoroughly with the cream, adding a little salt and pepper.

When tender, lift the bird(s) out of the casserole, carve and keep warm. Just before serving throw a lump of butter into a hot tureen or large, deep dish, add the mixture of eggs and cream and pour over it, very slowly, the juices from the casserole, stirring all the time; add the cooked vegetables and on top of them the carved bird(s).

Serve very hot with boiled rice and slices of brown bread comfortably buttered.

MARGARET CASSON

(Using a pressure cooker)

Serves 6

ILLUSTRATION BY **HUGH CASSON**

3 tablespoons butter

2-3 lb chicken, cut into pieces

1 medium onion

1 garlic clove

1 tablespoon flour

Rosemary and tarragon to taste

1 pint chicken stock

2 egg yolks

5 tablespoons yogurt

2 teaspoons cinnamon

Chopped almonds

Paprika

Warm 2 tablespoons of butter in the pressure cooker and brown the chicken pieces in it. Remove and keep warm. Put chopped onion and garlic in the butter and when cooked put back the chicken pieces and sprinkle with the flour. Mix together and add the herbs, then pour on the chicken stock. Close the lid, bring to high pressure, and cook for 10 minutes.

Remove the chicken to a casserole dish and boil down the juices in the pressure cooker to half the quantity. Check seasoning, then add to egg yolks beaten in a bowl. Put the yogurt in a separate bowl and add the cinnamon. Pour the juices and egg yolk mixture over the chicken, then spoon the yogurt on top. Sprinkle with chopped almonds and paprika.

DOMINIC DE GRUNNE

ILLUSTRATION BY **GREGG BECKER**

Choose plump birds, one per person; stuff them with grapes (green or red, or both; muscats are delicious). Bard them with streaky bacon. Brown in butter for a few minutes; squeeze on some grapes to add liquid; throw in a few more. Cook on a low flame for 30-40 minutes, turning over once or twice to cook evenly. Serve with vermicelli and extra-fine green peas, tinned if no fresh ones are available.

GUINEA FOWL WITH GRAPES

MAXIME ADAM-TESSIER

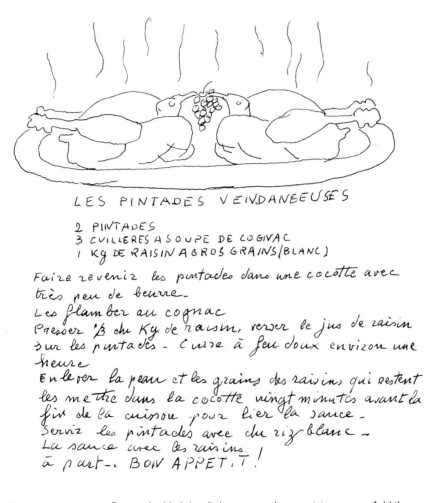

LES PINTADES VENDANGEUSES

2 PINTADES
3 CUILLERES A SOUPE DE COGNAC
1 Kg DE RAISIN A GROS GRAINS (BLANC)

Faire revenir les pintades dans une cocotte avec
très peu de beurre.
Les flamber au cognac
Presser 1/3 du Kg. de raisin, verser le jus de raisin
sur les pintades – Cuire à feu doux environ une
heure
Enlever la peau et les grains des raisins qui restent
les mettre dans la cocotte vingt minutes avant la
fin de la cuisson pour lier la sauce.
Servir les pintades avec du riz blanc –
La sauce avec les raisins
à part –. BON APPETIT !

2 guinea fowl
Butter
3 tablespoons cognac
2½ lb large white grapes

Brown the birds in a little butter in a casserole. Pour over the cognac and set it alight. Squeeze the juice from one-third of the grapes and pour it over the birds. Cover and cook over low heat for about 1 hour.

Remove skin and pips from the remaining grapes. Add the grapes to the casserole 20 minutes before the end of cooking time in order to thicken the sauce.

Serve the birds with boiled rice; hand round the grape sauce separately. *Bon appétit!*

CHRIS ORR

BREAST OF CHICKEN

2 chicken breasts, skinned

Tarragon

Butter

1 glass white wine

1 small tub single cream

SPICY POTATOES – CHRIS ORR STYLE

2 lb potatoes

Olive oil

3 teaspoons haldi (ground cumin from any Indian grocer)

BEANS AND TUNA DE LUXE

1 tin red kidney beans

1 small onion

2 garlic cloves

1 tin tuna in oil

Olive oil

Lemon juice

Pepper

Fresh mint leaves

MIXED SALAD

Watercress

A few carrots, grated

A few young leeks, cut into rounds

Endive

1 yellow pepper, sliced

Walnuts

Vinaigrette dressing

A Seduction Dinner

Prepare as much as you can at least 1 hour before the arrival of the seducee. Open the tin of red kidney beans and drain off the sludge. Chop up the onion and garlic and mix together with the tuna and olive oil, lemon juice and pepper. Put into a blue and white bowl and decorate with fresh mint leaves.

Peel the potatoes and boil them until they are nearly soft. Slice them thickly and put them into a frying pan with some oil and the haldi. Sauté until they have absorbed all the oil and are an even brown. They can be served hot or cold.

Cut the chicken breasts into small pieces, sprinkle with tarragon and sauté gently in butter. After a few minutes add the glass of wine and finally the cream. Ignore any protestations by your friend about this being heart-attack material. Say: 'I believe in having a good time now, and anyway tomorrow we might be run over.'

The mixed salad is the cadenza of the meal. Chuck in anything that grabs your fancy, but remember that colour balance is important. For that very special seduction I would use the selection listed above. Dress with a vinaigrette made with olive oil, white wine vinegar and Dijon mustard.

Serves 2

2 chicken breasts
1 tablespoon oil
1 oz butter
Salt
Pepper
¼ pint amontillado sherry
4 oz mushrooms, sliced
¼ pint double cream

Skin and bone the chicken breasts. Cover with greaseproof paper and beat as if you were Samson killing a Philistine; but a rolling pin will prove more efficacious than the jawbone of an ass.

Heat the oil and butter in a frying pan. Add the chicken breasts and brown on both sides. Season with salt and pepper, cover the pan and fry gently until cooked through. Remove breasts and keep warm in a serving dish.

Pour the sherry into the frying pan. Add the mushrooms and cream and cook until the sauce has reduced a little. Pour over the chicken breasts and serve.

JOANNE BROGDEN

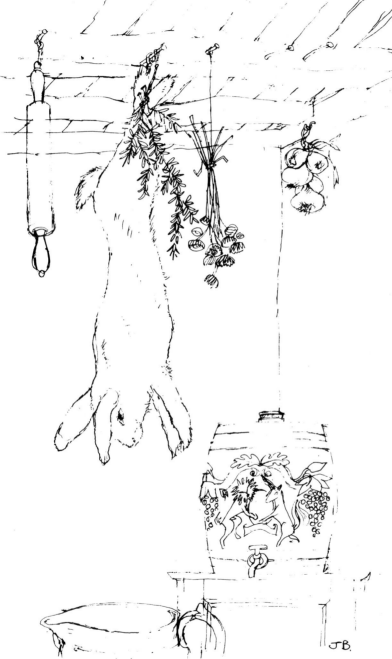

1 tame rabbit, about 3-4 lb
1 ½ lb onions
2 oz butter, plus a little olive oil
12 oz belly of pork, plus any scraps of smoked bacon, all diced
½ teaspoon salt
½ teaspoon coarse ground pepper
⅓ pint white wine
1 wineglass chicken stock
3 bay leaves
A sprig of rosemary
4 oz white mushrooms
2 teaspoons cornflour, potato flour or arrowroot

Take a fine rabbit, paunched and skinned, and joint it with a small sharp knife and small cleaver. If you do not have a cleaver use a carving knife on the bony parts and bang sharply with a wooden rolling pin. Jettison the lungs, but set aside the liver, heart and kidney.

Peel and slice the onions and soften in butter and oil in a frying pan; quickly done if you cover the pan with a lid. Have ready a warmed, fair-sized casserole – china, glass or metal (enamelled) – and as soon as the onions seem soft and golden, throw them into the casserole to make a bed.

Next, quickly fry the pork and bacon just to heat through and remove excess fat. Toss this on to the onions. Add salt and pepper, and pack in the pieces of rabbit neatly, preferably in one layer. Include the head and neck which will help to make a lovely firm stock. Add a little more salt and pepper. Have ready white wine (avoid cheap Spanish or Italian) and pour it over the rabbit. Add a good glass of chicken stock. If this amount of liquid looks too meagre, don't be afraid to add more stock or wine. Put in the bay leaves, and lastly a sprig of rosemary.

Cover the casserole and cook for 1 ½ hours. After 1 hour, throw in the mushrooms. Ten minutes before serving, thicken the sauce with the cornflour, potato flour or arrowroot, by removing some of the liquid and mixing it to a smooth paste with the flour. Test the rabbit with a pointed knife to see if it is done, then pour the flour mixture back into the casserole and gently stir it in.

Serve with petits pois, carrots and small potatoes baked in their jackets. This is a really delectable dish.

JOY LAW

ILLUSTRATION BY **EMMA CHICHESTER-CLARK**

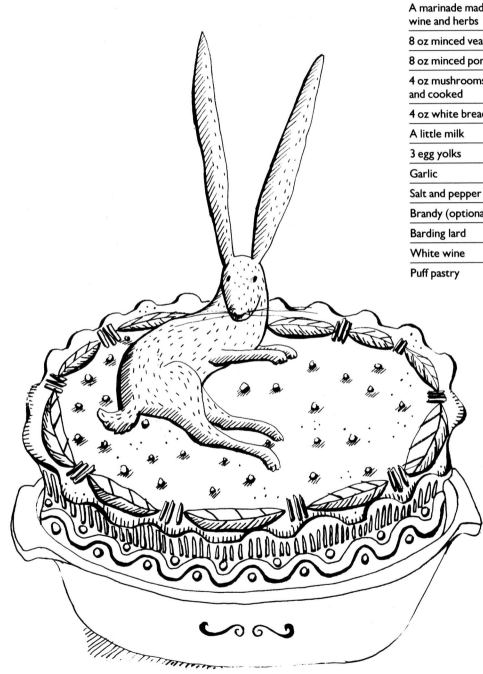

1 hare
A marinade made with red wine and herbs
8 oz minced veal
8 oz minced pork belly
4 oz mushrooms, chopped and cooked
4 oz white breadcrumbs
A little milk
3 egg yolks
Garlic
Salt and pepper
Brandy (optional)
Barding lard
White wine
Puff pastry

Do not attempt if the sight of blood makes you faint. Strip to the waist and bone a fine hare. Do not fret if you cannot get all the flesh away, as you will be able to salvage the clinging morsels once you have boiled up the bones to make a little stock.

Set aside the neatest pieces you have boned to marinate in red wine and herbs, and mince the messy bits and the liver with whatever you have now cleaned off the bones. Mix this with an equal quantity of minced pie veal and pork belly, the cooked mushrooms, the white breadcrumbs soaked in milk, 2 egg yolks, the blood of the hare, a little garlic and a good grinding of salt and pepper. A touch of brandy does not come amiss.

Lay strips of barding lard on a flat surface. Take pieces of the hare from the marinade, dry them on kitchen paper, then lay them on the bards. Cover with the stuffing moulded to shape, and finish off with another layer of hare. Bring the bards up round and tie firmly with kitchen string, making sure that the stuffing cannot ooze out.

Braise in a casserole in white wine for 1½ hours in a slow oven. Remove the cooked hare from the casserole, and let it cool.

Roll out the puff pastry to a shape large enough to enrobe the hare. Remove the string and barding lard and lay the hare sausage gently on the pastry. Close the pastry up, sealing it well, and glaze with the yolk of an egg. Bake in a hot oven for 35 minutes.

You need a rich gravy, a simple vegetable and perhaps a little apple sauce as an accompaniment.

PETER DE FRANCIA

An old recipe for cooking rabbit, much favoured by French peasants and poachers and evolved in pre-myxomatosis times when wild rabbits proliferated.

Shoot a rabbit. Skin it and cut it into pieces. Make a marinade of red wine, I tablespoon vinegar, a bouquet garni of thyme and bay leaf, I onion cut in quarters, salt and pepper, and marinate the rabbit for several hours before cooking.

Melt some bacon cut in squares in a small quantity of olive oil in a casserole. Sauté the well-dried pieces of rabbit until golden, adding a chopped onion. Add the marinade and let it reduce. Add 2 tablespoons flour and when this is thoroughly amalgamated add boiling water or stock. Cook gently until tender, seasoning as necessary.

Before serving remove the bouquet garni and add the liver which will have been cooked separately in a little oil or lard. Finally add the blood of the rabbit which you will have put aside, mixed with a small amount of vinegar. Do *not* let the sauce boil again.

Notes: The adding of the liver is not connected to any black magic ritual.

The blood mentioned in the final operation should only be that of the rabbit.

Dehydrated, tinned or Chinese frozen rabbit should only be used as a last resort.

Clean your shotgun after use.

MEAT

MAXIME ADAM-TESSIER

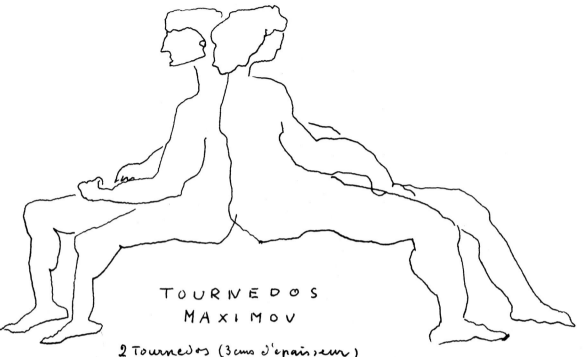

TOURNEDOS
MAXIMOV

2 Tournedos (3cms d'épaisseur)
Beurre - Champignons de couche
eminces - 1 yoghourt - 2 cuillères
à soupe de Dry Martini - Paprika

Cultivated mushrooms, sliced
Butter
I pot yogurt
Paprika
2 fillet steaks, about ⅛ in thick
Salt and pepper
2 tablespoons dry Martini

First fry the mushrooms in butter. Reduce the heat, add the yogurt, sprinkle liberally with paprika and stir well. Remove from heat and keep warm.

Fry the tournedos over high heat. Turn them, add salt and pepper, and remove them when cooked.

Deglaze the frying pan with the Martini diluted with a little water. Pour this over the tournedos and garnish them with the mushrooms.

BEEF AND PRUNES

SYBIL WALDOCK

ILLUSTRATION BY SUE SCULLARD

1 pint brown stock	
About 18 prunes	
1¼ lb chuck steak	
Seasoning	
1 oz flour	
2 oz fat or dripping	
1 tablespoon tomato purée	
2 bay leaves	
4 or 5 tomatoes	

Heat the stock, pour over the prunes and soak until tender. Dice the meat, roll it in seasoned flour and cook in the hot fat for a few minutes. Strain the stock from the prunes, add to the meat. Bring to the boil and cook until thickened. Add the tomato purée, about 6 finely chopped prunes and the bay leaves. Cover the pan and simmer for 1½-1¾ hours. Add the rest of the prunes whole and cook for a further 15 minutes. Skin tomatoes if wished, add to stew and cook for 14 minutes.

BRAISED STEAK WITH AUBERGINES

JEAN SOUTHWOOD

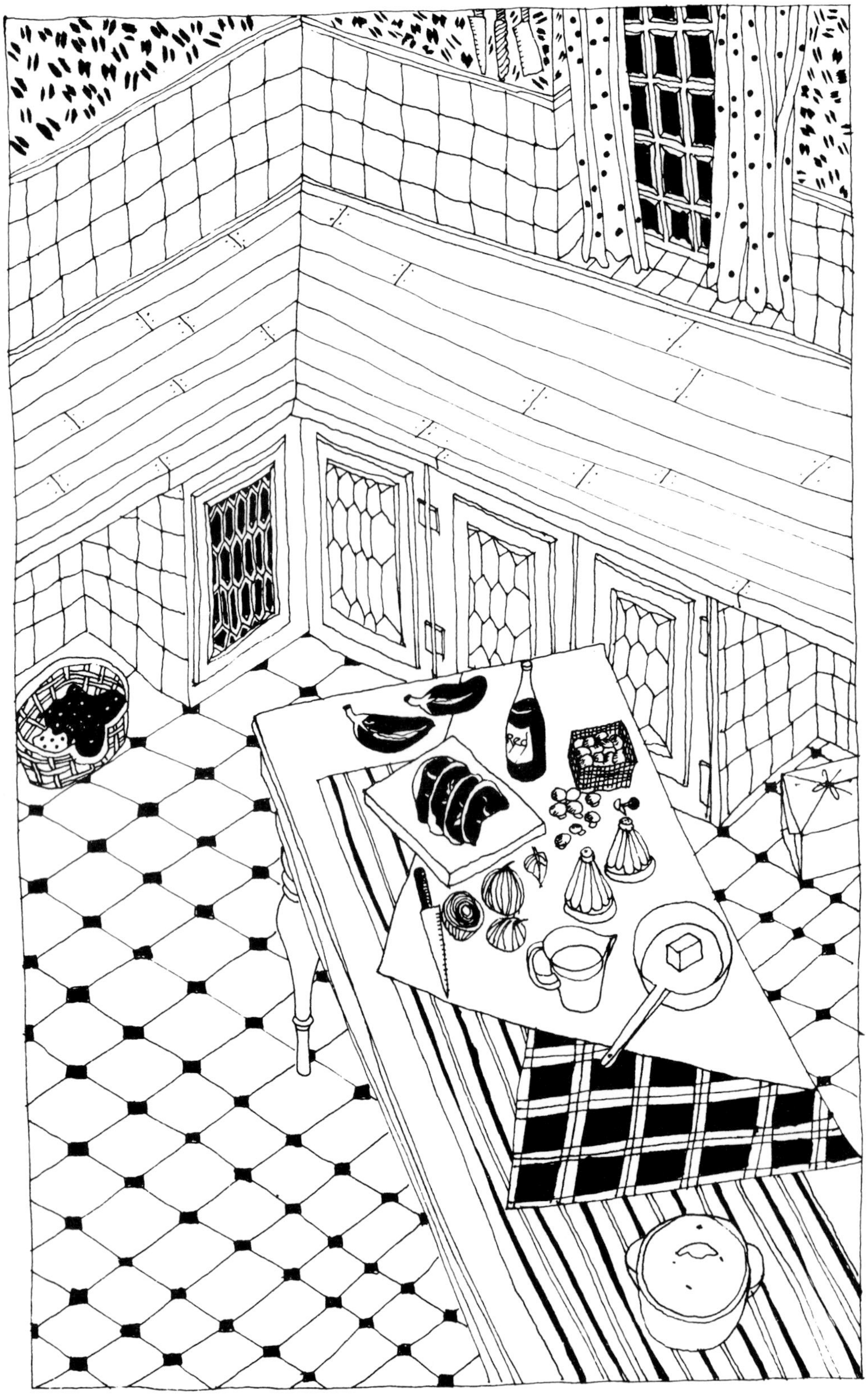

4 steaks for braising

Dripping

2 large onions, roughly peeled and chopped

8 oz mushrooms, washed and sliced

1 tablespoon flour

1 pint stock or stock and red wine

Bay leaf

Salt and pepper

2 aubergines, cut into ¼-inch-thick slices and sprinkled with salt

Brown the steaks on both sides in hot dripping in a flameproof dish or pan. Take out meat; put onions in pan and brown lightly. Add mushrooms, cook for a few minutes only, then dust in the flour. Remove the pan from the heat and add the liquid. Bring to the boil and add bay leaf and seasoning. Replace the steak. Cover the dish tightly and cook for about 1-1½ hours.

Wash the aubergines and drain, add to pan and cook until all the ingredients are tender. Sometimes it is necessary to remove the fat from the top of the casserole before serving.

ILLUSTRATION BY **CAMERON A. CAMPBELL**

HACHÉE

This traditionally Dutch, but nevertheless explosive dish, provides fun and food for all the family (except vegetarians). It is easy to cook and easy to eat, and takes you right back to the heart of the Low Countries. It warms those parts other stews do not, and is therefore recommended when it is time to put the skates on and when you feel hit by a windmill. I am not sure about the quantities required, but my advice is to make too much because it is even better a day or two later, warmed up and eaten with or on bread.

Serves 4

4 oz butter, plus a little lard
2 lb quality stewing beef, cut into cubes
About 2 lb wholesome onions, sliced
A little salt and pepper
Bay leaves
Cloves
Vinegar
Potatoes

Heat half the butter plus the lard in a frying pan and brown the meat on all sides. Transfer to a large saucepan or casserole.

Put the rest of the butter in the frying pan and brown the onions.

Put the onions with the meat. Season with salt and pepper and add a few bay leaves, some cloves and a spoonful of vinegar. Pour water over the lot, but not too much, and let it cook very slowly for at least 2 hours, covered with a lid.

Start cooking the potatoes near mealtime and serve them whole but crumbly with the hachée.

Eet smakelijk!

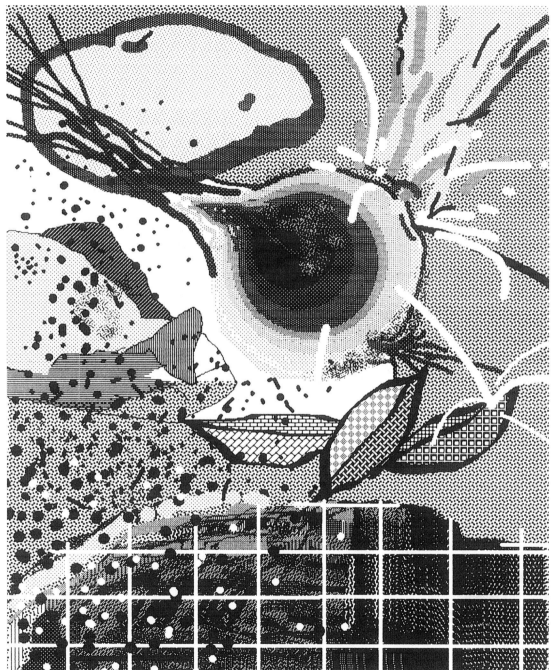

Hachée
Apple Computer

Floris van den Broecke
April 1986

FILLET OF PORK

DOSIA VERNEY

ILLUSTRATION BY **PETER LATHAN SMITH**

Rub the fillet with a mixture of salt, sugar, pepper and ginger in equal quantities. Fry quickly on all sides in hot fat. Lay in a deep casserole, on a bed of chopped onions and garlic, surrounded by mushrooms.

Pour over 1 tablespoon cranberry sauce, a tin of Buitoni's sauce, 1 dessertspoon sugar, some vinegar and ½ cup water. Add a bay leaf and cook slowly in the oven.

VALERIE LYONS

ILLUSTRATION BY **CHRISTINE SIMPSON**

4 pork chops

1 oz vegetable fat or lard

FOR THE SAUCE:

12 oz pineapple chunks

3 oz soft brown sugar

4 tablespoons vinegar

1 tablespoon soy sauce

¼ level teaspoon salt

2 level tablespoons cornflour

Place the pork chops in a roasting tin with the vegetable fat or lard. Put the tin just above the centre in a hot oven (200°C/400°F, gas mark 6) and brown for about 15 minutes, turning once.

Meanwhile, drain the pineapple from the can and reserve the syrup. Make the syrup up to ½ pint with water. Mix together the pineapple liquid, the sugar, vinegar, soy sauce and salt. Put the cornflour in a saucepan and moisten with a little of the liquid, mixing to a smooth paste. Stir in the remaining liquid and blend the mixture thoroughly. Place the pan over a moderate heat and cook, stirring all the time, until the mixture has thickened and is boiling. Add the pineapple pieces and draw the pan off the heat.

Remove the pork chops from the oven and drain off the excess fat from the roasting tin. Pour the sauce over the chops, coating each one thoroughly. Cover the tin with kitchen foil and replace in the oven. Lower the oven heat to 190°C/375°F, gas mark 5, and cook for a further 45-50 minutes according to the thickness of the chops, basting once or twice with the sauce.

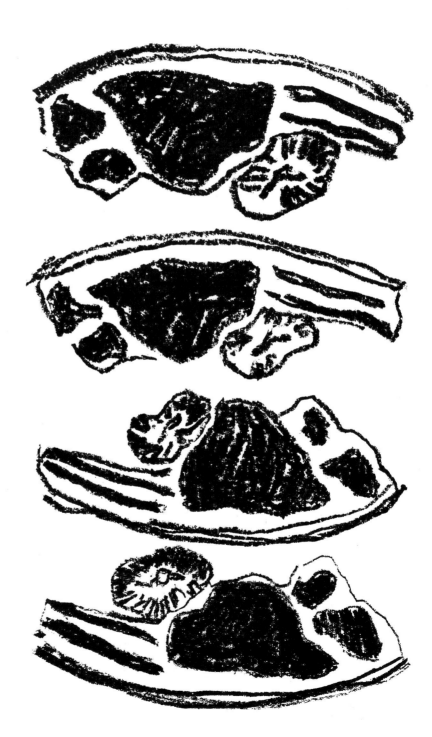

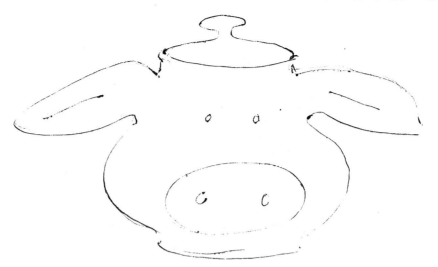

2 lb BELLY PORK
(CUT INTO 2" CUBES)

2½ TABLE SPOONS SOYA

1 LEVEL TEA SPOON SUGAR

2 CLOVES GARLIC

3/4 SLICES FRESH GINGER

2 FRESH CHILLIES OR
CHILLI POWDER

1 PINT OF WATER

BRING TO BOIL + SIMMER FOR
2 HOURS — SERVED WITH RICE +
GARNISH OF SPRING ONIONS

2 lb belly of pork, cut into 2-inch cubes
2½ tablespoons soy sauce
1 level teaspoon sugar
2 garlic cloves, crushed
3-4 slices fresh ginger
2 fresh chillies, or some chilli powder
1 pint water

Put all the ingredients in a pan and bring to the boil. Simmer for 2 hours. Serve with rice garnished with spring onions.

FRED DUBERY

Hot or cold Ham.

This is the way we cook a ham, so that it can be eaten hot or cold. A middle cut of gammon is best, but other less expensive joints like slipper or neck are very good.

Put a 2 or 3 lb piece of bacon into a heavy saucepan, fitting quite snugly, just cover with water, then add the following ingredients to make the pickle: 3 tablespoons of cider vinegar, 3 tablespoons of brown sugar, one teaspoon of cloves, one teaspoon of pepper corns, one small onion (about the size of a ping pong ball). A bouquet garni (fresh if possible). Simmer gently with the lid on, allowing 20 mins to the pound plus 20 mins, ie a 3 pound joint will take one hour & 20 mins. to cook.

To eat this hot, remove the ham from the pickle & serve with a cumberland sauce; vegetables could include lightly fried courgettes, buttered carrots, new or dauphinoise potatoes.

Before you sit down to eat this delicious supper, put the ham back into the pickle, leave it there to sit in a cool place for 24 hours. The joint can then be taken out of the saucepan, the skin removed, and if you wish the fat may be coated with breadcrumbs in the traditional manner. By returning the ham to the pickle you will ensure that it will remain succulent to the very last slice

This is the way we cook a ham, so that it can be eaten hot or cold. A middle cut of gammon is best, but other less expensive joints like slipper or neck are very good.

Put a 2-3 lb piece of bacon into a heavy saucepan (it should fit quite snugly). Just cover with water, then add the following ingredients to make the pickle:

3 tablespoons cider vinegar
3 tablespoons brown sugar
1 teaspoon cloves
1 teaspoon peppercorns
1 small onion (about the size of a ping-pong ball)
A bouquet garni (use fresh herbs if possible)

Simmer gently with the lid on, allowing 20 minutes to the pound, plus 20 minutes – i.e. a 3 lb joint will take 1 hour 20 minutes to cook.

To eat this hot, remove the ham from the pickle and serve with Cumberland sauce. Vegetables could include lightly fried courgettes, buttered carrots or new potatoes.

Before you sit down to eat this delicious supper, put the ham back into the pickle. Leave it in a cool place for 24 hours. The joint can then be taken out of the pan, the skin removed and if you wish the fat may be coated with breadcrumbs in the traditional manner. By returning the ham to the pickle you will ensure that it will remain succulent to the very last slice.

JOY LAW

ILLUSTRATION BY **SUSAN HILTON**

| I leg of lamb, boned |
| Chopped onions |
| Mushrooms |
| 3 lambs' kidneys |
| Butter |
| Salt and pepper |
| Any herbs that go well with lamb |
| Puff pastry |
| I egg yolk |

If you cannot bone the leg of lamb yourself, get the butcher to do so, but ask him not to sew it up or string it.

Cook the chopped onions, mushrooms and kidneys in a little butter. Mix well with the herbs and seasoning. Put this stuffing into the leg of lamb and sew up tidily. Bake for 30 minutes at a good heat (220°C/425°F, gas mark 7), then remove from the oven.

When quite cool envelop the joint carefully in puff pastry, making sure that you have sealed all the edges. Brush with egg yolk. Bake for a further 30 minutes in a hot oven and serve immediately.

You need a sharp carving knife, and a rich brown gravy to which some port has been added to earn salvos of praise. Plain boiled potatoes and a crisp salad make good accompaniments.

LAMB STEW

8 lamb chops, trimmed

2 oz butter

1½ lb small potatoes, halved

4 oz small button onions

8 oz mushrooms, chopped

5 fl oz white wine

½ pt white stock

2 oz white breadcrumbs (optional)

5 fl oz cream

Salt and pepper

1 bay leaf

A sprig of thyme

A sprig of parsley

A sprig of rosemary

Chopped parsley

Fry the chops in butter, then remove from the pan. Put the potatoes, onions and mushrooms in the pan and cook for 5 minutes. Lift out the vegetables; drain the fat from the pan, then add the wine, stock, breadcrumbs and cream. Stir thoroughly and season to taste.

Return the vegetables and chops to the pan with the herbs. Cover and simmer for about 1 hour or until tender. Remove the bay leaf, sprinkle chopped parsley over the top and serve.

JOAN CATLIN

This is a cheap, north-east country lunch dish which was traditionally made on wash days, as the housewife could prepare it and leave it to cook in the oven while she attended to the laundry.

ILLUSTRATION BY **CAROLYN GOWDY**

1 large Spanish onion

Salt

Pepper

1 good-sized potato per person

1 slice of bacon per person

1 sausage per person

1 tomato per person

Put on the oven at 180°C/350°F, gas mark 4. Slice the onion and lay it in a roasting tin. Add salt and a good grinding of pepper. Slice the potatoes thinly and lay these on top. Arrange the bacon slices and sausages next, and the tomatoes cut in half. Grind some more pepper over the tomatoes. Cook in the oven for 45 minutes.

RUSKIN SPEAR

The finest haggis is found near the Gateway to the Trossachs, near Aberfoyle. Foyle is the early Celtic spelling for foil – foil being an absolute must when steaming the haggis, which should be in perfect condition with an unbroken skin. Wrapped in foil, no water must be allowed to penetrate the haggis. 'Bashed neeps', or turnips as we call them, complete the dish, except for a modicum of Black Label, or some prefer 'Red Hackle' (obtainable in Glasgow but not in Edinburgh).

Remember to stick to this recipe and you cannot foil.

Eat while standing with your back to the wall leaving your sword arm free.

MARTA ROGOYSKA

Bigos is a traditional Polish dish and the word simply means bits and pieces mixed together. It is a popular main dish, eaten with rye bread or potatoes, and used to be taken on hunting expeditions because it gets better with every reheating, and most important, it warms the system in cold weather. There are almost as many variations on this dish as there are Poles in the world, but this is our favourite recipe.

ILLUSTRATION BY PER DAHLBERG

Take the same amount of raw white cabbage as sauerkraut (which will need rinsing to reduce bitterness if from a tin or jar). Chop the white cabbage very finely into strips. Cook both the cabbage and the sauerkraut over low heat in two separate pots (not aluminium as sour ingredients react badly with this metal) until the cabbage is soft. Add salt and a little water if no liquid is produced within the first few minutes. Stir constantly. When the cabbage is soft, mix both into a large pot and add:

Any left-over meat, chopped into cubes

Polish garlic sausage, diced

Bacon, ham, etc

A whole dried wild mushroom

Bay leaves

Caraway seeds

A few whole peppercorns

A couple of juniper berries, if available

All of this mixture has got to cook well over a low heat, and needs constant stirring for at least 1 hour. Then taste and add salt if necessary.

Finally, add a glass of red wine and at least a couple of tablespoons of 'Powidla' (Polish plum spread). Taste again and adjust seasoning and ingredients if necessary. It should then be ready to serve. It can be prepared a few days in advance, or it can be made in a vast quantity and eaten slowly over a longish period as this dish definitely improves as time goes by.

VEGETABLES

L U T Z   B E C K E R

German cookery is particularly well known for its excessive use of potatoes. In the provinces of Saxony and Thuringia they use an old recipe for potato dumplings which is unique in this world and I shall give it to you, without hesitation.

The Thuringian dumplings are a glorification of the potato. They formed part of the traditional Sunday lunch for the large families of the nineteenth century — and what an occasion it used to be. The entire family was involved, helping in the kitchen.

Serves 8

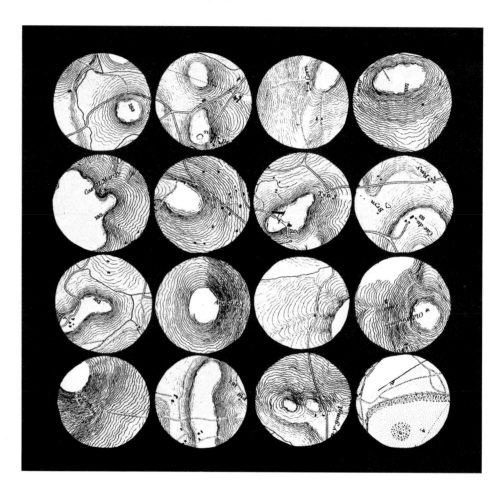

5½ lb large potatoes, peeled

2 cups boiling milk

1½ tablespoons salt

1 pinch nutmeg

8 oz bread cubes

Butter

Grate two-thirds of the potatoes with a sharp, rough grater. Put the pulp into a linen cloth and squeeze the water out. Both grating and squeezing are quite hard work and the male guests should be employed for this. (The drier the pulp, the better the dumplings will be.)

Boil the remaining potatoes in salt water, then mash them, and stir the boiling milk into them. Finally, mix them into the raw potato pulp. Knead the mixture well and add salt and nutmeg. Fry the bread cubes in butter. Take a good handful of the potato mixture, press one or two croûtons into its centre and form the dumplings between your hands. Make them the size of a large snowball and press them firmly together. Throw the dumplings into boiling salt water and cook them over a low flame for approximately 15 minutes.

The Thuringian dumplings are best eaten with game, goose, beef and plums, and are terribly good with red cabbage.

I doubt that you will have any dumplings left over, but if you have, they are delicious warmed up. You cut them into slices and fry them in butter. My last advice is: make enough of them. Your guests' appetites will develop while eating, to an incredible degree.

RÖSTI

DAVID QUEENSBERRY

Rösti is excellent with roast game and is very popular with children.

PHOTOGRAPH BY **JULIA HEDGECOE**

1½ lb potatoes, peeled
Butter and oil
Salt
Pepper

Parboil the potatoes for 7 minutes, drain and leave to cool. Put in the refrigerator for several hours or overnight. This makes a difference to their texture which affects the finished dish.

Grate the potatoes, using a coarse grater. Heat a mixture of butter and oil in a non-stick frying pan and sprinkle with salt and pepper. Spread the grated potato evenly in the pan and sprinkle with a little more salt and pepper. Put a plate of appropriate size upside down over the potatoes. The plate should fit in the pan, not sit on top of it. Cook gently for 10 minutes.

To turn the rösti out of the pan, put a wooden board over the plate and pan, then turn the whole thing over. If the pan is very dry, add a little more butter and oil, then slide the rösti back into the pan and cook the other side for 10 minutes. Turn out in the same way. You now have a circular potato cake sitting on the plate, ready to be cut into slices.

SYBIL WALDOCK

Serves 4

ILLUSTRATION BY SARAH HOLLAND

1½-2 lb aubergines
Salt
6 slices white bread, crusts removed
1 lb tomatoes
8 oz Cheddar cheese
3 oz cooking fat
Pepper

Wash and slice the aubergines, sprinkle with salt and leave in a colander for 30 minutes to draw out moisture.

Meanwhile, toast the bread, skin and chop the tomatoes and grate the cheese.

Pat aubergines dry and fry lightly in the fat until golden on both sides. Place the toast in a shallow ovenproof dish. Cover with layers of aubergines, cheese and tomatoes, sprinkling with salt and pepper to taste. Repeat layers, finishing with cheese, and bake at 190°C/375°F, gas mark 5, for 30-40 minutes.

YEHUDI MENUHIN

ILLUSTRATION BY BLAISE THOMPSON

4 large aubergines

Salt

2 onions, finely chopped

4-6 oz mushrooms, thinly sliced

Butter

4 large ripe tomatoes, skinned, seeded and chopped

1 tablespoon tomato purée

Marjoram

Thyme

Oregano

2 garlic cloves, crushed

½ pint stock

5-6 chopped anchovy fillets

Some stoned black olives

3 oz brown breadcrumbs

3 oz grated Gruyère cheese

2 tablespoons chopped parsley

Olive oil

Cut the aubergines in half, lengthwise; scoop out the pulp leaving the shells intact. Salt and drain the shells for about 30 minutes, then rinse and dry carefully.

Fry the onions, aubergine pulp and mushrooms gently in some butter till very soft. Add the tomatoes, the purée and the herbs, garlic and stock, stirring well, and finally the anchovies and olives.

Mix the breadcrumbs, cheese and parsley in a bowl, then add the cooked tomato mixture. Paint the skin of each aubergine shell with olive oil, then fill the shells with the stuffing. Bake in a covered dish in a moderate oven until the shells have softened and are cooked through.

M Y F A N W Y   P I P E R

I ate this dish in an Italian restaurant some years ago and have never seen it on a menu since, or found it in any cookery book – so this is an improvisation. The pine kernels are my own addition.   Serves 4

ILLUSTRATION BY J O H N P I P E R

4 medium fennel bulbs

About 4 oz cooked, chopped spinach

About 4 oz cream cheese or home-made yogurt cheese (but *not* cottage cheese, which is tasteless and grainy)

Black pepper

Salt

1-2 tablespoons pine kernels

About 4 tablespoons tomato sauce (this should be fresh and well reduced)

Cut the fennel bulbs in half and put in a pan in one layer, cut side up. Barely cover with salted water. Bring to the boil and cook until tender (about 20 minutes if they are fairly young). Drain and reserve the water.

Scoop out some of the centre of each fennel bulb and chop. Put in a bowl with the spinach and cheese and mix well. If using a food processor do not reduce the mixture to a paste. Season with pepper. Taste and add salt if necessary.

Add the pine kernels and mix again or return to the processor.

Put a generous spoonful of the mixture on each fennel half and top with the tomato sauce. Serve hot or cold. (If you are serving it hot, thin the tomato sauce with a spoonful or two of the fennel cooking liquid and pour over the fennel before heating the dish in the oven.)

GEORGE HOWARD

This is a Castle Howard recipe which we have had for years; it can be served at lunch time or as a first course for dinner.

ILLUSTRATION BY **QUENTIN BLAKE**

4 heads of whole, well-washed lettuce

3 oz finely chopped onion

2 oz butter

1 tablespoon cornflour

½ pint good brown gravy

Pepper and salt

Cook the lettuce until tender, saving ¼ pint of the cooking liquid. A pressure cooker gives the best result. Keep the lettuce hot. Now cook the onion in butter until brown, add cornflour, cook for 1 minute, then add gravy and lettuce liquid. Stir until it thickens a little, season with pepper and salt. Coarse or sea salt is best for the seasoning. When very hot, pour over warm lettuce and serve at once.

KENNETH ARMITAGE

Parsnips are often maltreated or ignored. They need butter and careful attention. For this recipe, high quality sausage of the Cumberland type is essential – meat and no rusk, or very little. There are fine sausages made in Cheltenham too, which are sold by good grocers and occasionally fishmongers in the Cotswolds and in the West of England. Alternatively, minced belly of pork can be used.

6 parsnips

Butter

1 lb sausages or belly of pork

Thyme

¾ pint cheese sauce

3 tablespoons grated Gruyère or Parmesan or well-dried-out Cheddar

2 oz fresh breadcrumbs

2 tablespoons melted butter

Peel and slice the parsnips and boil until just tender (remove any hard core first). Place half in a buttered gratin dish. Scatter with the skinned and crumbled sausages, or minced belly of pork. Add plenty of butter and some thyme. Put the remaining parsnips on top. Pour the cheese sauce on top and sprinkle with the cheese and breadcrumbs and the melted butter. Bake in a moderate oven until browned and bubbling. Complete browning under the grill, if the oven has to remain low for other dishes.

ILLUSTRATION BY **SIMON PHILLIPS**

VEGETABLE TERRINE

JOY LAW

This recipe sounds very unlikely to succeed or even taste nice, but faith is required. It is a heavenly dish and will earn accolades not only because it is delicious but because it looks so well designed.

8 oz green beans

6 artichoke hearts

8 oz new carrots

8 oz fresh or frozen peas

8 oz ham

1 egg white

Pepper

Salt

2 tablespoons ground nut oil

Juice of 1 lemon

10 vineleaves

Cook the vegetables until just tender and drain well. Cut into appropriate slices.

Chop the ham and refrigerate it and the mixer-bowl for 30 minutes. Put the ham, egg white, pepper and salt into the mixer and gradually add the oil and lemon juice. You must do this very quickly so that the paste does not get hot. Line the bottom and sides of an 8-inch rectangular bread tin with 8 of the vineleaves and then a layer of the ham paste. Lay carrot roundels, peas, 1 inch lengths of bean and sliced artichoke hearts on the bed of ham paste and cover with another thin layer of the paste. Put a second row of vegetables in and cover with a lid of ham paste and 2 vineleaves. Bake in a warm oven for 30 minutes.

Leave the terrine to get cold for at least 8 hours before turning it out. Serve with a tomato sauce, spiced with vinegar, tarragon and parsley.

GRATIN DAUPHINOIS

ROBIN LEVIEN

1½ lb potatoes

1 garlic clove, crushed

Freshly grated nutmeg

Salt and pepper

½ pint double cream

1½ oz butter

Parsley

Thinly slice the potatoes (easy with a mandoline) and wash and dry them. Put in layers in a gratin dish, sprinkling each layer with garlic, nutmeg, salt and pepper. Pour in the cream, fleck the top with butter and cook at 150°C/ 300°F, gas mark 2, for 1½ hours. Sprinkle with chopped parsley. Excellent with steak.

ILLUSTRATION BY **PAUL COX**

J O H N B R A T B Y

The most beautiful baked beans I have ever tasted – cooked by Mick Arnup ARCA.

When I was a ragged student, kicked out of Kingston Art School, I had a friend, a painting student, but far more successful than I was, who lived in digs at the top of a hill on the way to Surbiton. At night, penniless and hungry, I would knock on his door.

'Come in, you old sod Bratby,' he would say with a mixture of scorn and perhaps a modicum of affection. We would climb to the top of the house.

He would then prepare a frying pan and in it melt real butter, as he toasted pieces of bread. Into the real butter – the clue to this feast – he would pour Heinz baked beans from a tin. Having cooked the beans he would anoint pieces of buttered toast with them.

'There you are, you old bugger,' he would say, plonking down the plate. My delight defies description.

ALF DUNN

Select one large potato per person. Peel the potatoes and slice them lengthwise into strips – they should be ½ inch wide and ½ inch thick.

Heat some oil in a chip pan until approximately 190°C/375°F, or until a test chip sizzles fiercely when dropped in the oil. Place the chips in a chip basket and cook at full heat for a few minutes, then turn to half heat for about 5-10 minutes. When the chips seem nearly cooked turn heat up to full again and sprinkle liberally with garlic salt.

While the chips are cooking, cut slices of granary bread and spread thickly with butter.

Drain the chips and fill the sandwiches, sprinkling them with salt and vinegar. A good sandwich should be more chips than bread and should ooze butter when bitten. Serve with a glass of beer.

PUDDINGS

ROXANNE'S KALAMAZOO BANANA SPLIT

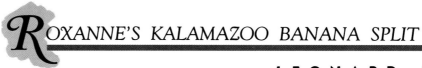

LEONARD ROSOMAN

Serves 1 as a main course or 6 as a starter.

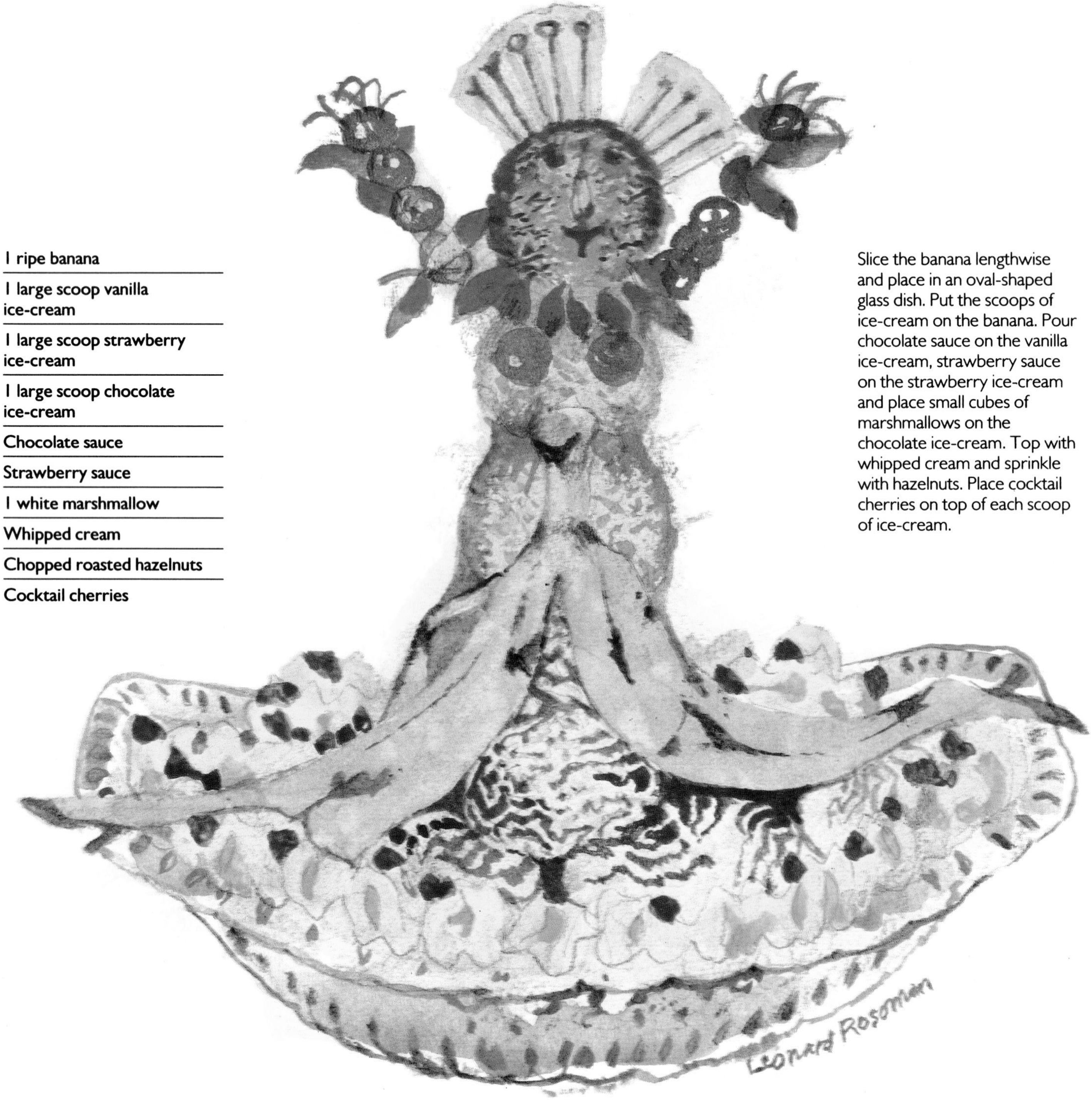

- 1 ripe banana
- 1 large scoop vanilla ice-cream
- 1 large scoop strawberry ice-cream
- 1 large scoop chocolate ice-cream
- Chocolate sauce
- Strawberry sauce
- 1 white marshmallow
- Whipped cream
- Chopped roasted hazelnuts
- Cocktail cherries

Slice the banana lengthwise and place in an oval-shaped glass dish. Put the scoops of ice-cream on the banana. Pour chocolate sauce on the vanilla ice-cream, strawberry sauce on the strawberry ice-cream and place small cubes of marshmallows on the chocolate ice-cream. Top with whipped cream and sprinkle with hazelnuts. Place cocktail cherries on top of each scoop of ice-cream.

BOBBY GILL

FOR THE APRICOT JELLY:

8 oz dried apricots

Rind and juice of 1 lemon

½ oz gelatin

½ pint double cream, lightly whipped

FOR THE AMARETTO JELLY:

4 egg yolks

3 oz castor sugar

¾ pint milk

3 oz ground almonds

2 tablespoons Amaretto di Saronno

½ oz gelatin

½ pint double cream, lightly whipped

First make the apricot jelly. Put the apricots in a pan, add the pared lemon rind and juice, cover with water and cook until soft. Purée the fruit and leave to cool.

Soak the gelatin in 2 fluid oz water and dissolve over heat. Add the whipped cream to the apricot purée and fold the gelatin into the mixture.

Next make the Amaretto jelly. Beat together the egg yolks and sugar until pale. Bring the milk to the boil, whisk into the egg yolk mixture and return to the pan. Cook over a low heat, stirring continuously until the custard thickens. Whisk in the almonds and Amaretto. Leave to cool.

Soak the gelatin in 2 fluid oz water and dissolve over heat. Add the gelatin to the almond mixture. Stir from time to time and when the mixture begins to thicken, fold in the whipped cream.

When the apricot and almond mixtures are half set, pour alternating layers (½-1 inch deep) into an oiled 2½-pint mould. Leave to set in the refrigerator.

DONALD AND JUDY HAMILTON FRASER

1 large peach per person

6 oz can frozen orange juice concentrate

2 oz flaked almonds

Immerse peaches in boiling water so that the skins slip off easily. Cut in half and remove the stones. Arrange cut side down in an ovenproof dish.

Dilute the frozen orange juice with only half the recommended quantity of water. Pour over the peaches and sprinkle with the flaked almonds. Bake for 20 minutes in a moderate oven (170°C / 325°F, gas mark 3).

Serve hot or cold, preferably accompanied by a glass of champagne.

KRYSIA BROCHOCKA

ILLUSTRATION BY **CATHY NOBLE**

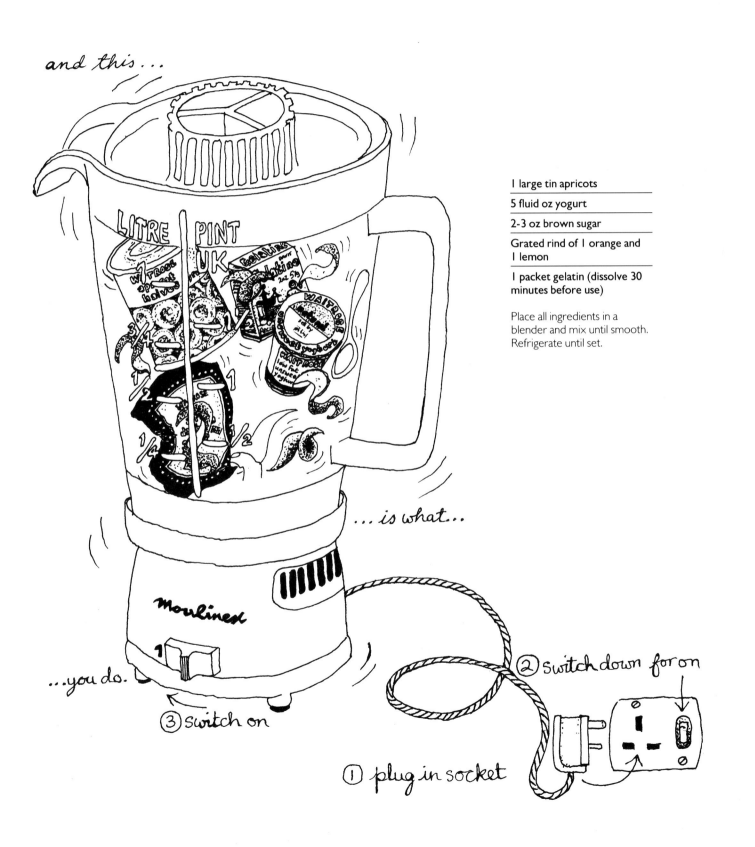

and this...

...is what...

...you do.

③ switch on

② switch down for on

① plug in socket

1 large tin apricots

5 fluid oz yogurt

2-3 oz brown sugar

Grated rind of 1 orange and 1 lemon

1 packet gelatin (dissolve 30 minutes before use)

Place all ingredients in a blender and mix until smooth. Refrigerate until set.

Peel, halve and stone ripe
Italian peaches. Halve and pip
large black grapes. Place in a
bowl and cover with a
generous quantity of Vecchia
Romagna or similar brandy.
    Leave the fruit to soak for
2 hours before serving.

BERNARD MYERS

The faintly bitter, burnt taste of the roasted nuts and the smoky taste of the tea give this fruit salad a distinctly autumnal flavour.

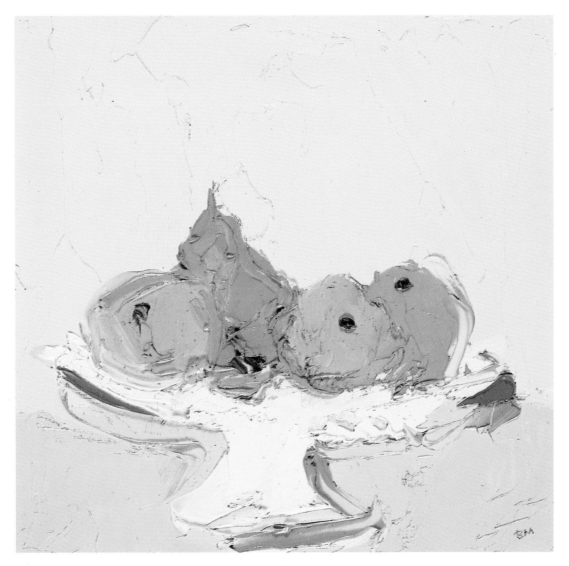

| 4 oz seedless raisins |
| 3 oz hazelnuts |
| 2 grapefruit |
| 3 oranges |
| 3 bananas |
| 3 tablespoons freshly made Keemun jasmine tea |
| 4 tablespoons chunky orange marmalade |
| 4 tablespoons Kirsch |

Soak the raisins in lukewarm water for 2 hours.

Lightly roast the hazelnuts in an oven preheated to 150°C/300°F, gas mark 2, for about 10 minutes. Shake them occasionally. As soon as their skins turn brown and start flaking off, take the nuts out of the oven and rub off the remaining skins with a clean, dry cloth.

Peel the grapefruit and oranges and carefully remove all the pith. Divide the grapefruit into segments and skin them with a sharp knife. Slice the oranges into thin rounds. Peel and slice the bananas.

Drain and dry the raisins. Put them into a serving bowl with the fruit and nuts.

Make the tea. Heat the marmalade with the tea and Kirsch in a small saucepan. Pour over the fruit, mixing carefully with a fork. Chill for at least 6 hours, but for maximum flavour do not serve straight from the refrigerator.

NATASHA SPENDER

ILLUSTRATION BY **GARY McCARVER**

4 oz butter

5½ oz castor sugar

3½ oz ground almonds

3 egg yolks and 3 egg whites

1½ oz flour

Strawberries

Almonds

Icing sugar

Cream the butter and sugar and beat until white. Then add the ground almonds, egg yolks and flour. Lastly whip in stiffly beaten egg whites. Put in a shallow buttered cake tin and cook for 30-40 minutes at 180°C/350°F, gas mark 4.

When cool, pile strawberries on top, stick almonds into the pile of strawberries, and sprinkle icing sugar over the top.

Serve with puréed raspberry sauce. Alternatively, serve strawberries and purée together in a glass dish and serve the cake separately cut into fingers. If the alternative method of serving is used, it is better to cook the base in a square cake tin as it is then easier to cut into fingers.

1 lb strawberries

2 lb rhubarb, wiped clean

1 tablespoon powdered gelatin

4 oz castor sugar

Sieve ½ lb of the strawberries and set aside.

Cut the rhubarb into pieces. Put in a saucepan with ¼ pint water and simmer until very soft. Cool slightly, then liquidize.

Pour half the rhubarb purée into a saucepan and heat gently, then dissolve the gelatin in it, stirring constantly. Transfer the mixture to a large bowl. Add the remaining rhubarb purée and the sugar, and stir until the sugar has dissolved completely. Finally, add the sieved strawberries and mix thoroughly.

Pour the mixture into a wetted mould and put in the refrigerator. When the jelly has set, serve surrounded by the remaining whole strawberries.

ILLUSTRATION BY **HANNAH FIRMIN**

3 large cooking apples

3 large oranges

3 oz brown sugar

FOR THE TOPPING:

1 oz margarine

2 tablespoons Golden Syrup

4 oz porridge oats

1 teaspoon ground cinnamon

2 oz brown sugar

Peel, core and slice the apples. Peel the oranges and break into segments. Mix the apples, oranges and sugar together and put in an ovenproof dish.

Melt the margarine and syrup in a saucepan. Take the saucepan off the heat and add the porridge oats, cinnamon and sugar. Mix together and then place this mixture on top of the apples and oranges and bake in the oven (180°C/ 350°F, gas mark 4) for 1 hour until golden and crisp.

This pudding is delicious served with sour cream.

*S*UE'S APPLE BRÛLÉ

DAVID GENTLEMAN

For a while each autumn we enjoy a lovely profusion of apples from my wife's parents in Norfolk. The windfalls are used to make this lovely pudding.

Make a thick purée, not too sweet; put it in a fireproof dish (it should be about three-quarters full) and stroke the purée flat. Add ¼-½ inch of very dark brown sugar, making sure there are no lumps, and again stroke it flat. Grill it, watching all the time; it is done when it bubbles and glistens. Set aside to cool, then put in the fridge. When it is cold, the top should be hard, like toffee. Serve with cream.

SPRING PUDDING

2 lb. Rhubarb, 3 Tbsp Lemon juice,
1½ lb Sugar
Thin slices White bread
> Whipped cream

Cut rhubarb into 1 inch segments.
Combine rhubarb, lemon juice
and sugar in a saucepan,
bring to the boil stirring continuously,
lower heat and simmer until
rhubarb becomes soft. Don't let
rhubarb disintegrate entirely.
Trim crusts from bread, cut each
slice in half lengthwise and
line sides of soufflé dish, cut
enough triangles to cover bottom,
fill with rhubarb mixture, reserving
some of its juice to pour over,
topping of more triangles, chill
in fridge overnight, cover with
whipped cream before serving.

2 lb rhubarb

3 tablespoons lemon juice

1 lb sugar

Thin slices white bread, crusts removed

Whipped cream

Cut the rhubarb into 1-inch chunks. Put in a pan with the lemon juice and sugar and bring to the boil, stirring continuously. Lower the heat and simmer until the rhubarb is soft but not completely disintegrated.

Cut several slices of bread in half and line the sides of a soufflé dish. Cut the remaining slices into triangles and line the bottom of the dish. Fill with the rhubarb mixture, reserving some of the juice. Cover with more bread triangles and pour the reserved juice on top.

Chill in the fridge overnight and cover with whipped cream before serving.

BERNARD NEVILL

ILLUSTRATION BY **KRISTIN JAKOB**

1 lb strawberries

1½ lb sharp cooking gooseberries

½ lemon

½ breakfast cup demerara sugar

Wash the fruit well, hull the strawberries and top and tail the gooseberries. Place in a deep saucepan and cover with water to 2 inches above the fruit. Add the squeezed lemon juice, then cut the skin into quarters and add to the fruit with the sugar and bring to the boil. Simmer gently for 30 minutes, stirring occasionally to ensure the fruits are blended together. Turn into a fruit dish, cool and place in refrigerator. Serve ice cold with fresh clotted cream and 'Brontë' shortbread.

(Comtesse Guy de Toulouse-Lautrec)

4 oz bitter chocolate, broken into pieces

6 oz castor sugar

4 oz unsalted butter

2 egg yolks

½ pint Kirsch (or Cointreau)

12 oz sponge fingers

½ pint double cream

Melt the chocolate in the top of a double boiler. Stir to a smooth paste with a wooden spoon. Remove from the heat, stir in half the sugar, the butter, the egg yolks, and half the Kirsch. Mix thoroughly.

Butter a charlotte mould or cake tin.

Mix the remaining Kirsch with an equal amount of water. Dip each sponge finger in the mixture and put a layer of fingers on the bottom of the mould, then a layer of the chocolate mixture. Alternate the layers until the mould is filled, ending with a layer of fingers. Chill in the fridge for several hours.

To turn out, dip the mould in hot water for a few seconds, turn out onto a serving dish and serve covered with whipped cream sweetened with the remaining sugar.

ROBERT BUHLER

Grind through a mincer, slowly and evenly to ensure a smooth texture. For really large parties, a larger moose is better – it goes further.

X BARS OF CHOCOLATE
MIX TO TASTE

1. MOOSE
= CHOCOLATE MOUSSE.

MOUSSE

SYBIL WALDOCK

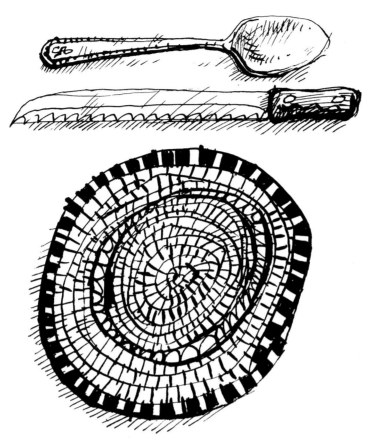

ILLUSTRATION BY **BLAISE THOMPSON**

1 lb stale bread, brown or white
3 oz brown sugar
4 oz sultanas, currants or raisins
1 tablespoon self-raising flour
2 oz shredded suet
2 teaspoons mixed spice
Grated rind and juice of 1 lemon

Soak the bread, then squeeze to get rid of surplus moisture. Place in a bowl and add all the rest of the ingredients. Mix well together and place in a greased basin. Cover with greaseproof paper and steam for 2½ hours.

Alternatively, put in a tin, cover with greaseproof paper and bake in the oven at 150°C/300°F, gas mark 2, for 1 hour. Remove paper and bake at 200°C/400°F, gas mark 6, for a further 15 minutes or until golden brown. Leave in the oven for a few minutes after turning off the heat. Turn out on a plate and sprinkle with sugar.

THEO CROSBY

FOR THE PASTRY:

6 oz flour

3 oz butter or margarine, cut into pieces

1 oz castor sugar

1 oz icing sugar

3 egg yolks, lightly beaten

Vanilla essence, to taste

FOR THE FILLING:

1 cup milk

1 teaspoon butter

3 tablespoons sugar

1½ tablespoons cornflour

1 egg, lightly beaten

Cinnamon

Sift the flour into a large bowl. Make a well in the centre and add all the other pastry ingredients. Mix the butter, sugar, egg yolks and vanilla essence together, drawing in the flour a little at a time. When all the flour has been incorporated, flatten the dough with your hand, then draw it up again. Repeat several times, then leave the dough to rest for 30-40 minutes.

Meanwhile, make the filling. Put the milk and butter in a pan and bring to the boil. Add the sugar. Mix the cornflour with a little water and add to the boiling mixture. Cook gently until it thickens, then stir in the beaten egg.

Roll out the dough and use it to line a flan dish. Add the filling, dust with cinnamon and bake in a fairly hot oven for about 25 minutes.

REG GADNEY

Not a recipe for the faint-hearted or the penny-pincher – it takes a good afternoon to master and a lot of what you've got in the way of patience; very beautiful, unpredictable, expensive, sweet and capable of producing such gasps of pleasure that cautious men have been known to ask for cheese instead.

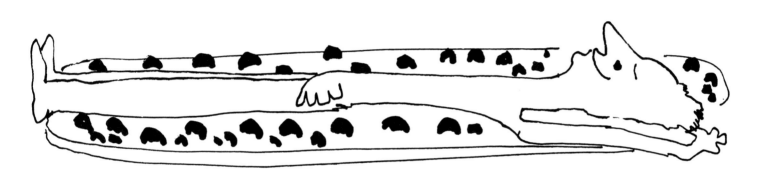

PASTRY
Use a cake tin that has a false bottom so you can get your pastry mould out at the end. Make up a sweet and short pastry. For a 10-inch tin use 1½-2 cups of flour (all-purpose). Put flour in a bowl, stir in a generous tablespoon granulated sugar and a pinch of salt. Make dough with 6 tablespoons fat, a bit less of butter and 2 tablespoons vegetable shortening with 3 tablespoons water and 1 of lemon juice. Set in the tin and bake at 200°C/400°F, gas mark 6, for about 10 minutes, till brown. Set aside on a cooling tray, so that the air can get all round the pastry case, to avoid sogginess.

CREAM FILLING REGINALD
Put 1 cup granulated sugar and 6 egg yolks in a bowl and beat with electric whisker until the mixture is firm and just flowing. Add a cup of well-sifted flour and whisk again. Beat in 1½ cups boiling milk very gradually indeed. Pour the mixture into a saucepan and bring to the boil, stirring constantly. Reduce the heat and cook gently for 3-4 minutes. Put on side of stove and add a glob of butter, 2 teaspoons vanilla essence and 4 teaspoons cognac. Stir.

ASSEMBLY
Smear Cream Filling Reginald into pastry case carefully. Then pack strawberries on top of the filling. Use the smaller tastier kind. Boil up some redcurrant jelly and use this to glaze the strawberries so that everything glitters. Do not put the tart in the fridge, but watch out for flies or any early visitors who might be tempted to have a nibble before whoever is turning up to share the tart turns up.

The only thing you can drink with this is very cold Champagne. I've tried every variation of this procedure, including the recipe given by Simone Beck, Louisette Bertholle and Julia Child, but mine is the best. And you'll be surprised how many people fight to get in through the door when you say you've got a French tart sitting on the fridge.

BRIAN SMITH

Design Researchers add silicon chips and small currents

Fashion Designers like it with turnups and potatoes in their jackets.

Industrial Designers add nuts and bolt it down

Painters find adding greens suits their palates

2 eggs
Butter
Milk
1 tablespoon flour
At least 1 tablespoon muesli

The faint-hearted mix the ingredients to a batter in a bowl, pour in pan and cook. The bold add the ingredients direct to the pan with creative abandon. Eat with pepper, salt, chutney or jam.

MARGARET CASSON

ILLUSTRATION BY **HUGH CASSON**

3 oz plus 1 tablespoon castor sugar
2 eggs
½ pint milk

To be made in a pressure cooker.

First make the caramel. Put 3 oz sugar in a small heavy saucepan and cook over low heat until golden brown. Add 1 tablespoon water and stir for a few seconds while it continues to cook. Pour into a lightly oiled 1-pint soufflé dish.

Beat the eggs in a bowl. Heat the milk and pour over the eggs. Stir in 1 tablespoon sugar. Pour into the soufflé dish with the caramel in the bottom, cover with foil and place the dish in the basket or on the stand in the pressure cooker with ½ pint water. Close the lid, bring to high pressure, and cook for 8 minutes. Remove the dish and when cool put in the fridge for a few hours. Turn out and serve with cream.

JOAN CATLIN

ILLUSTRATION BY EMMA CALDER

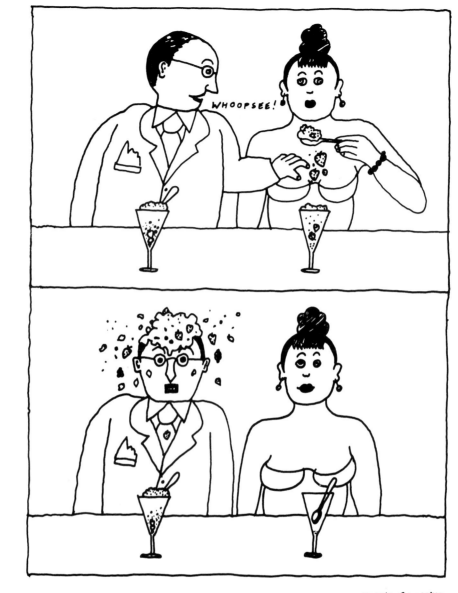

½ pint double cream

Juice of 1 lemon

1 tablespoon grenadine or pure raspberry syrup

Lashings of brandy or sherry

1 drop vanilla essence

Whisk everything together. Serve chilled in wine glasses on a cushion of wild raspberries, strawberries or sliced peaches and spiked with blanched almonds.

GERALD BENNEY

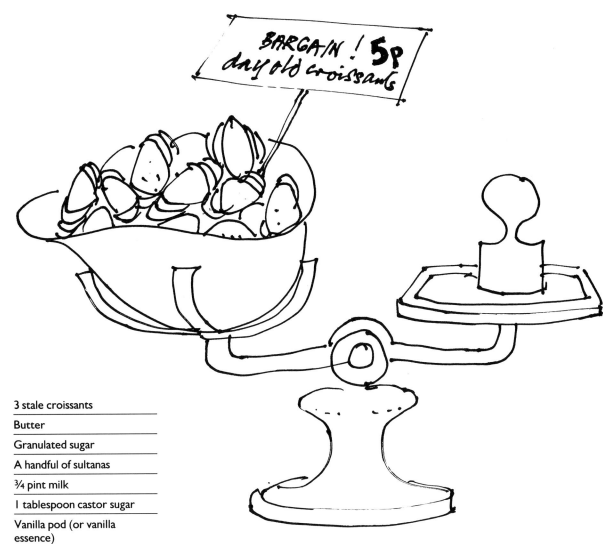

3 stale croissants

Butter

Granulated sugar

A handful of sultanas

¾ pint milk

1 tablespoon castor sugar

Vanilla pod (or vanilla essence)

2 eggs, beaten in a bowl

Slice croissants lengthways into thin slices. Place in layers in a buttered dish, scattering each layer with a little sugar and a few sultanas. The croissant slices do NOT need buttering.

Make a custard by bringing the milk, sugar and vanilla pod (or a little vanilla essence) to the boil. Remove vanilla pod and pour the milk onto the eggs. Stir and pour over the croissants. Sprinkle with sugar and set in a bain-marie. Cook in moderate oven until the top is brown and crusty. Serve hot.

Great Great Grandmother's Christmas Pudding

| 10 oz muscatel raisins |
| 2 glasses wine or brandy |
| 3 oz currants |
| 8 oz shredded suet |
| 8 oz breadcrumbs |
| 8 oz syrup – golden and black |
| 1 teaspoon allspice |
| ¾ pint milk |
| 3 oz candied peel |
| Silver coins |

Mix everything well. Put into pudding basin, cover with greaseproof paper and pudding cloth and boil for 2 hours. Boil for a further 2 hours when required for use.

KENNETH IRELAND

ILLUSTRATION BY MICHAEL FOREMAN

10 oz flour

½ teaspoon salt

5 oz butter

6 oz plus 2 tablespoons castor sugar

2 oz chopped walnuts

2 tablespoons iced water

4 large pears, peeled, halved and cored

1 egg white, lightly beaten

5 fluid oz double cream, stiffly whipped

First make the pastry. Sift the flour and salt into a large mixing bowl. Add the butter and rub into the flour with your fingertips until the mixture resembles coarse breadcrumbs. Mix in 4 oz of the sugar and 1½ oz finely chopped walnuts. Add the iced water with your fingers, mix and knead the dough. Wrap the dough in greased paper and chill in the refrigerator for 30 minutes.

Meanwhile, make the filling. In a medium-sized saucepan dissolve 2 oz sugar in 5 fluid oz water over low heat, stirring constantly. When the sugar has dissolved, boil syrup for 4 minutes. Add pear halves, reduce heat and simmer for 10-15 minutes or until pears are tender. Set aside to cool. Preheat the oven to 190°C/ 375°F, gas mark 5.

On a lightly floured board, roll out two-thirds of the dough into a circle large enough to line a 9-inch flan tin. Gently ease the dough into the flan tin and trim off any excess dough.

Remove pears from the pan and arrange them, narrow ends towards the middle and cut sides down, in the dough case. Dampen the edges of the dough. Roll out remaining dough into a circle large enough to fit over the top of the tart. Using your fingers, gently press the dough edges together.

With a pastry brush, brush the top of the dough with the egg white and dust with 2 tablespoons castor sugar. Bake for 30-35 minutes. When cold, serve with whipped cream sprinkled with the remaining chopped walnuts.

JOCELYN STEVENS

8 oz butter

8 oz castor sugar

2 eggs, beaten

4 oz self-raising flour

1 teaspoon mixed spice

12 oz sultanas (or raisins)

Zest and juice of 1 lemon

4 fluid oz milk

4 tablespoons golden syrup

ILLUSTRATION BY **ED DAY**

OUT OF THE STRONG COMES FORTH...

Cream butter and sugar until pale and fluffy. Beat in eggs, then fold in flour, spice, sultanas and lemon zest and juice. Bind with milk.

Turn into a greased pudding basin and cover with greaseproof paper or foil. Tie on securely. Steam for 2½ hours.

Turn out, pour the golden syrup on top and serve at once.

CAKES AND BISCUITS

DOSIA VERNEY

ILLUSTRATION BY NICHOLAS HARDCASTLE

1 lb dried fruit	Soak the dried fruit and brown sugar overnight in the cold tea. Add the egg and self-raising flour. Mix well. Cook in a greased loaf tin for 1½-2 hours at 150°C/300°F, gas mark 2.
1 cup brown sugar	
1 cup cold tea	
1 egg, well beaten	
2 cups self-raising flour	

ANNE MORLEY

8 oz digestive biscuits

8 oz dessert chocolate

8 oz butter

2 eggs

3 oz castor sugar

Small glass of brandy (or rum)

2 oz walnut halves

2 oz glacé cherries

Crush the biscuits coarsely. Melt the chocolate with the butter over a very low heat. Beat the eggs and sugar together until creamy, then beat in melted chocolate and butter. Fold in the crushed biscuits, the brandy, 1 ½ oz walnuts and 1 ½ oz cherries. Put in buttered mould or small cake tin. Decorate with the remaining nuts and cherries. Refrigerate until 30 minutes before serving.

ILLUSTRATION BY **LUCY DUPRE**

CASSATA ALLA SICILIANA

ALAN FLETCHER

Drink a glass of Bonzy champagne with a slice of Cassata alla Siciliana

1 lb ricotta cheese	
10 oz castor sugar	
Maraschino (optional)	
At least 4 oz bitter chocolate, broken into small pieces	
At least 4 oz candied peel, chopped	
4-6 oz light sponge cake	
Icing sugar	

Sieve the ricotta cheese into a bowl; add the sugar and whip until creamy. Add maraschino to taste. Add the chocolate and candied peel.

Line a high-sided pie dish with greaseproof paper. Cut the sponge cake into ½-inch slices, and line the sides and bottom of the dish.

Pour some maraschino on to the sponge slices. Pour the creamed ricotta mixture into the sponge case and smooth the top. Cover with the remaining sponge slices.

Put the dish in the fridge for a few hours or overnight. Turn out on to a serving plate and dust with icing sugar.

ᗷLACK CHOCOLATE CAKE

This is a serious cake for the truly obsessed choc-o-phile. It is dark and strong with a hint of bitterness, and there is a satisfying mixture of sponge and filling. Definitely keep out of the reach of children.

4 oz self-raising flour, sifted

1 level teaspoon baking powder

4 oz castor sugar

3 large fresh eggs

4 oz soft margarine

2 generous tablespoons sieved cocoa powder

1 generous tablespoon ground cinnamon

2-3 tablespoons milk

A pinch of salt

FOR THE TOPPING AND FILLING:

6 oz semi-sweet plain chocolate

5 oz sour cream

2 tablespoons brandy, if wished

Walnut halves

Preheat oven to 170°C/325°F, gas mark 3.

Grease and flour a cake ring, 9 inches in diameter. Put all the cake ingredients into a mixing bowl and beat thoroughly, either by hand or with an electric whisk, till smooth. Spoon the mixture into the cake ring and bake for 25-30 minutes. When the cake is cooked, allow it to cool for a few minutes before turning it out on a wire rack.

To make the topping, break the chocolate into a bowl, set over a saucepan of simmering water, add the cream and stir until the chocolate is melted. Allow to cool.

Cut the cake into 2 rounds and sprinkle with brandy. Sandwich with half the chocolate cream and spread the rest on top. Decorate with the walnut halves.

R O G E R   N I C H O L S O N

"Gunpowder Cake"

An incredible receipe for a cake. Almost the best I have eaten Very economical. A War time receipe. Icing & Gunpowder optional according to taste.

SIEVE TOGETHER:

1 ½ cups self-raising flour
1 cup sugar
1 teaspoon bicarbonate of soda
2 tablespoons cocoa

MELT:

5 oz margarine
2 tablespoons vinegar!
1 cup warm water
A splash of vanilla essence

Mix everything together, put in a well-greased cake tin and cook at 190°C/375°F, gas mark 5, for 45 minutes.

JEAN SOUTHWOOD

ILLUSTRATION BY **MEL CALMAN**

1 cup rolled oats	
1 cup plain flour	
½ cup brown sugar	
¼ teaspoon baking soda	
½ teaspoon baking powder	
½ cup butter	
FOR THE FILLING:	
½ lb stoned dates	
3 tablespoons brown sugar	
Juice of ½ lemon	

First make the filling. Boil the dates with ½ cup water, the brown sugar and the lemon juice. Cook until soft and leave to cool.

Now make the cake. Mix the dry ingredients, then rub in the butter. Place half the mixture in a cake tin, cover with date filling, then press the remaining half over the filling. Bake in a moderate oven for 23-30 minutes.

4 oz flour

4 oz cornflour

4 oz castor sugar

4 oz butter

1 large egg, beaten

Sift the flour and cornflour into a bowl, add the sugar and then rub in the butter. Add the egg and make into a dough. Roll out thinly on a floured board.

Cut animal shapes out of thin cardboard. Place on top of the rolled-out dough. Cut round the shapes with a sharp knife.

Bake in a moderate oven (190°C/375°F, gas mark 5) until biscuit coloured – about 12 minutes.

Decorate the biscuits.

HILARY C. WATSON

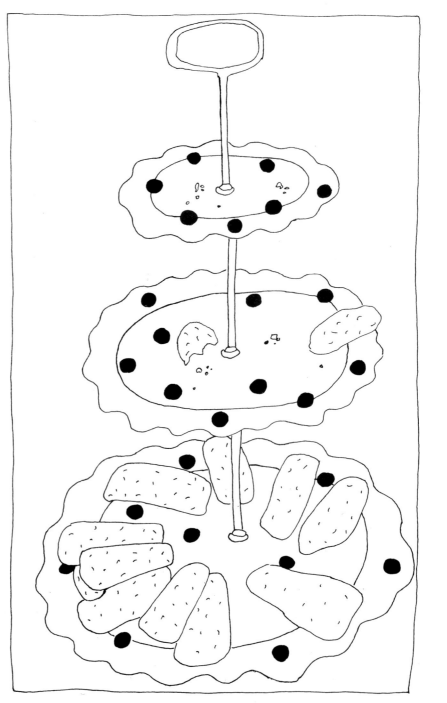

ILLUSTRATION BY SIOBHAN NOONAN

4 oz butter (or 2 oz butter, 2 oz margarine)

4 oz sugar (the finer the better, but granulated will do)

8 oz self-raising flour

Switch on oven at 180°C/350°F, gas mark 4.

Place butter in a pan and melt over a gentle heat. When the fat has melted, add the sugar. Stir the mixture until the sugar has melted. Turn the heat to very low and sieve the flour into the mixture, making sure it is well stirred together.

When all the flour is sieved into the mixture, you should have a dough, rather than a runny syrup. Place this between two pieces of greaseproof paper and roll the mixture out. Without paper, the mixture will set like concrete on board and rolling pin.

Cut into biscuit-sized pieces and place on a greased baking tray. Cook in oven till very pale gold in colour – about 12-15 minutes.

CHUTNEYS, SAUCES

AND OTHER

DELIGHTS

JOY LAW

ILLUSTRATION BY **GILL BRADLEY**

2 large onions, finely chopped or minced

1 lb stoned dates, finely chopped

16 ripe bananas, sliced or mashed

8 oz crystallized ginger, chopped

Salt

Pickling spices

Wine vinegar

1 lb black treacle

Put the onions, dates, bananas and ginger into a large saucepan or preserving pan, with 1 tablespoon salt and the pickling spices in a bag and add vinegar just to cover. Boil for 5 minutes. Remove the pickling spice bag, add the black treacle, and cook gently for 20 minutes, stirring constantly. Pot while the chutney is still hot.

CHRISTOPHER FRAYLING

'Steady the buffs!' muttered Sergeant 'Big' Mac under his breath, as he strove to keep the final jar of the regimental chutney at arm's length from the hungry kings of the forest.

It was one of those everyday occurrences which called for decisive action on his part.

With a single bound, he was free – by the simple and simultaneous expedient of trapping the Giant Python, emasculating the Ravenous Tiger, and silencing the Imperial-looking Lion.

'Just as well!' mused Mac, 'for if I had mislaid the precious jar of chutney, what was left of me would certainly have been drummed out of the Regiment.'

Actually, he need not have exerted himself, for did he but know it, the Commanding Officer had persuaded a trusty old elephant to memorize the recipe – down to the last detail. . . .

SGT. MACLAGLEN, ON HIS WAY BACK TO BARRACKS WITH THE REGIMENTAL CHUTNEY, SURPRISED BY THE KINGS OF THE FOREST. . . .

1 lb dates	
1 lb large raisins	
2 lb apples	
2 lb brown sugar	
4 oz preserved ginger (or root ginger)	
4-6 garlic cloves	
1 teaspoon cayenne	
1 tablespoon salt	
1 quart malt vinegar	

Chop the dates and raisins; core and chop the apples.

Put in a bowl with all the other ingredients and leave to soak overnight.

Next day, pour the mixture into a preserving pan, bring to the boil, and simmer for 1 hour. Mustard seed, wrapped in muslin, can be added to the mixture for extra sharpness.

For regimental quantities, multiply the ingredients by 5 or 10, and requisition a platoon of empty jars.

Ideal with cold meat, cheese and, of course, curries.

The sort of chutney, dear reader, on which the sun never sets.

RICHARD GUYATT

Robin Darwin was particularly proud of the way he made this traditional recipe for mayonnaise (he once gave a talk on it for *Woman's Hour*). He always stressed that the secret of the art lay in the patient beating of the mixture, with a wooden spoon, until that critical point is reached when the sauce, if turned upside down in its mixing bowl, remains firm, defying the law of gravity.

On one of his visits to Castle Howard he persuaded his hosts to allow him to invade the kitchens and make the mayonnaise for the dinner party that evening. He excelled himself in his efforts.

When, that evening, it was at last offered to him, he could not resist the impulse of snatching the sauceboat off the tray, springing to his feet and performing an impromptu pirouette of triumph round the table, bringing his dance to a climax by demonstrating the test over his head. Disaster struck! He had failed to realize that while a ceramic surface grips, a silver one slithers. . . .

Makes enough for 6 good helpings

3 egg yolks
½ teaspoon salt
Tarragon vinegar
Lemon juice
½ pint olive oil

Put the egg yolks in a bowl and stir thoroughly. Add the salt, a drop or two of tarragon vinegar and a squeeze of lemon. Then add the oil, drop by drop with great care, gently accelerating the pace of stirring – which must be done with a wooden spoon – as the mixture thickens.

Add drops of vinegar from time to time, again with delicacy as there is a risk of ruining the consistency of the sauce if too much is added.

Keep stirring with a gentle rhythm until the mixture is thick and firm enough to withstand the Darwin test.

Note: an extra touch. Add very finely chopped chives to make the sauce a light green colour, or a few drops of Tabasco to suffuse it with pink.

JOAN CATLIN

ILLUSTRATION BY **GREGG BECKER**

8 oz sugar
½ cup water
½ tablespoon butter
1 tablespoon treacle
1 tablespoon vinegar
6-8 eating apples, spiked on cocktail sticks

Put the sugar, water, butter, treacle and vinegar into a saucepan over low heat. Once the ingredients have melted together, bring to the boil, *without stirring*. Boil until cracking point is reached: test by taking a teaspoon of toffee and dropping it into a glass of cold water. When ready, the toffee should form a stiff thread which cracks.

Twirl the apples quickly in the toffee and set on a buttered dish to cool.

ROBERT GOODDEN

Quinces, peeled and cored

Granulated sugar

Icing sugar

Put the quinces into a preserving pan and add water to three-quarters of their depth. Cook gently until the fruit is very soft, then strain and force through a sieve.

Measure the quince purée and add an equal volume of granulated sugar, combining the two in the preserving pan. Cook rather gently, stirring often, until the mixture has passed through a volcanic stage (kitchen gloves, long-handled spoon), has taken on a deep rosy-amber colour and begins to come away from the sides of the pan. It takes quite a long time, so be patient. Spoon the thick purée on to shallow oiled baking dishes and leave to cool.

When quite cold and set into a firm jelly, cut into mouthful-sized squares, roll in plenty of icing sugar and store. The candy keeps at least until the New Year.

ILLUSTRATION BY HANNAH FIRMIN

TERRY FROST

8 large black olives, stoned

Sea salt

Charcoal grill the olives on a skewer until spitting hot. Remove from the grill and sprinkle liberally with salt.

Place 3, 5 or 8 hot olives in the mouth. The resulting explosion clears the head. Follow this with a glass of ouzo and continue your journey to Aphrodite with clarity.

To enable lovers of Ouzo to get their second wind & continue their journey to Aphrodite

LEMON CORDIAL

JOAN CATLIN

COOL AND REFRESHING
with that extra little bite

ILLUSTRATION BY **ANN MARSHALL**

2 lemons
½ oz tartaric acid
12 oz granulated sugar

Grate the rind from the lemons, then slice the lemons thinly. Put the lemons, rind, tartaric acid and granulated sugar into a large jug. Pour on 2 pints of boiling water and stir until the sugar has dissolved. Leave to cool.

Serve chilled, diluted to taste.

SHEILA ROBINSON

I cook as seldom as possible,
but I do need marmalade —
Take 30 Seville oranges, four lemons,
   wash, put the whole fruit into a pan,
   cover with water, simmer until tender,
   pour the lot into a bowl, until the next day.
Put 12 lbs preserving sugar into the pan,
   the sliced fruit, separating the pips.
   6½ pints liquid, adding water if there is
   not enough from the first simmering, pips—
   tied in muslin, boil gently, stirring, test
   after 2½ hours, cool, pot, cover,
All this makes about 20 lbs of marmalade — or more.
                                        SK.

Makes about 20 lb marmalade

30 Seville oranges

4 lemons

12 lb preserving sugar

Put the washed fruit in a pan, cover with water and simmer until tender. Pour the lot into a bowl and leave until the next day.

Slice the fruit and put the pips in a muslin bag. Put in a pan with the sugar and 6½ pints liquid (use the reserved cooking liquid, adding more water if necessary to make it up to the correct amount). Boil gently, stirring regularly for about 2½ hours or until setting point is reached. Leave for about 10 minutes before potting in warmed jars.

ILLUSTRATION BY **GARY McCARVER**

BUTTERSCOTCH SAUCE

¾ cup brown sugar

I cup corn syrup

½ cup butter

I cup single cream

Put the sugar, corn syrup and butter in a pan and heat until the sugar has dissolved. Add the cream and bring to the boil.

BITTER CHOCOLATE SAUCE

4 oz bitter chocolate

½ oz castor sugar

2 fluid oz whipping cream

2 oz butter

6 tablespoons milk

Melt the chocolate. Put the sugar, cream, butter and milk in a pan and bring to the boil, then add the melted chocolate. Bring everything to the boil again, then pour into a bowl and beat while it cools.

MARS BAR SAUCE
Melt one Mars bar per person and ladle over vanilla ice-cream.

PAUL HUXLEY

It was August 1964. I had found a fellow addict, we were sitting in Schrafft's on East 57th Street and I was about to be introduced to one of their hot chocolate fudge sundaes. Iced water stood in perspiring tumblers on the counter. It was all laid out for us.

Then followed the biggest trauma in my two-year stay in America. The chocolate mirages hardly hit the counter before my friend complained:

'No chipped nuts I said!' – and without a pause both orders were slopped down the waste disposal.

Anyone raised in wartime Britain like me is a high-risk candidate for chocolaholism. I got it early. Mars bars, petit pot au chocolat, Schwarzwälder Kirschtorte, they're all kids' stuff – eventually you have to main-line. For me it's hot chocolate sauce – black, sinister, and not too sweet. Here's how you do it:

Ladle a couple of dollops of golden syrup into a saucepan, add about the same amount of cocoa powder and a splash of water. Heat and stir until hot and dissolved. Add a pinch of salt.

Pour the hot sauce over a generous serving of chocolate chip ice-cream. Sip cold water between mouthfuls.

PETER DE FRANCIA

ILLUSTRATION BY **LESLIE JOHNSON**

The recipe is so simple and the results so tempting that there appears to be no reason why bottled fruit in alcohol could not become the main home-based craft activity involving the greater part of the population. Fruit is plentiful. There is only one snag involved: getting hold of the alcohol. Customs and Excise laws in Britain, and regulations governing distilleries, make things difficult. Hence the mysterious disappearance of Applejack (Calvados) since the eighteenth century. Fearsome legislation punishes those brave enough to set up illicit stills. A close friendship with doctors or chemists does not help: surgical spirit is too strong. Meths should be avoided as a substitute, even by fanatics.

Jars are needed, preferably with heavy screw tops. The best kind are those with a wire clip fixture, sealed by a flat rubber band.

The best fruit to bottle are cherries, especially the red varieties, but greengages, apricots, small peaches and large grapes of the kind known as Dattier (usually available in mid-September) are also excellent. Cherries and grapes should have their stalks cut, leaving about a quarter of an inch on the fruit. This facilitates their being eaten between finger and thumb. All other fruits should have their skins pierced by a needle. Approximately ten jabs are made on an average-sized greengage. This is to enable the alcohol to penetrate the fruit. Peaches, unless very small, should be halved. A jumble of all kinds of fruit impatiently shoved into the jars is to be discouraged. Known as 'Confiture de vieux garçons', this system is only legitimate when used by those over the age of 80.

The fruit – which should not be overripe – is placed in the jars, carefully packed but not rammed down. Approximately 2 dessertspoons of castor sugar are added to an 8-inch jar. The alcohol, roughly 45 degrees in strength, is poured over the fruit, which should be completely covered. The liquid should not touch the rubber band, leaving about quarter of an inch of air space between the surface and the lid. The lid is then sealed tightly.

Following this operation nothing is required except patience. A minimum of one year should elapse before the fruit is ready. Greediness is to be discouraged. The contents of the jars change colour over this period, and the fruit tends to darken. Two competing schools of thought exist concerning the ideal place to store the jars. The first insists that these should be placed in a cupboard away from light. The second propounds the view that they should be placed on shelves and that light is beneficial to the maturing process. Long experience has shown that there is not the slightest difference between the two theories.

The fruit is eventually ladled into glasses and either eaten with a spoon, or in the case of cherries or grapes, by the stalks. The liquid is drunk and is often far better than expensive brandy.

My great great great great great grandfather, Jean Guille, kept a notebook in 1780 of recipes he used for the family business of producing cordials and waters. He had left France for England some years earlier.

The French grade their liqueurs by their consistency, sweetness and alcoholic strength into *crèmes, huiles* and *baumes* which are of thick oily consistency, and *eaux,* extracts or elixirs which are less sweet and limpid. All have a base of either some tasteless high-proofed alcohol, or for a superior concoction, brandy, whisky or rum, plus a sweetener such as sugar, honey or syrup, and the flavouring of herbs, seeds and so on. They are made either by distillation or maceration, which means leaving everything to soak in the alcohol, filtering and racking off, much like making wine but without the fermentation. So cordials and waters by maceration come under the heading of *eaux,* extracts or elixirs.

Jean Guille used brandy almost exclusively. A gallon of brandy before the end of the eighteenth century cost less than a guinea – say around 24p for a litre bottle. If you are not prepared to make a hogshead of 53 gallons, which all his recipes are for, you will need to divide his quantities by 241 if you only want to make 1 litre.

The notebook contains 21 recipes. Some of them are called by their main flavour, Cinnamon, Clove, Mace, Fennel and so on. Others have more exotic names. Who could resist Oil of Venus or True Love Water? Wormwood Water could be a challenge. Absinthe contained wormwood – said to drive men mad – and it is now illegal to manufacture it in Europe and the United States.

OIL OF VENUS
Makes 1 hogshead

1 lb caraway seed	
4 oz mace	
4 oz clove	
8 oz ginger	
8 oz cinnamon	
1 noggin essence of lavender	
8 oz essence of cedrat	
7 oz saffron	
40 lb sugar	
49 gallons brandy	
4 gallons water	

(Cedrat is a variety of lemon; a noggin is ¼ pint)

FENNEL WATER
Makes 1 hogshead

6 lb fennel seed	
1 lb iris of florence	
1 lb liquorice	
35 lb sugar	
43 gallons brandy	

TRUE LOVE WATER
Makes 1 hogshead

3 oz mace	
3 oz cinnamon	
3 oz clove	
8 oz coriander seed	
1 noggin essence of cedrat	
40 lb sugar	
8 oz cochineal	
2 oz alum	
42 gallons brandy	
11 gallons water	

FLORENCE'S FAVOURITE
Makes 1 hogshead

1 lb mace	
1 lb caraway seed	
½ noggin essence of lemon	
40 lb sugar	
40 gallons brandy	
13 gallons water	

MACARONI CORDIAL
Makes 1 hogshead

3 lb bitter almonds	
4 oz caraway seed	
2 oz angelica seed	
8 oz clove	
1 lb coriander seed	
1 noggin essence of cedrat	
40 lb sugar	
49 gallons brandy	
4 gallons water	

WORMWOOD WATER
Makes 1 hogshead

10 lb wormwood	
8 oz caraway seed	
8 oz cinnamon	
40 lb sugar	
49 gallons brandy	
4 gallons water	

MARGARET CASSON

ILLUSTRATION BY **HUGH CASSON**

I always keep a couple of tins of Buitoni ratatouille ('poor stew . . . bad stuff . . . mess' – French dictionary) on my shelves, so that when I have some left-overs such as cold meat, chicken, ham or fish, I can produce a delicious meal in hardly longer than it takes to open one of the tins.

Cook a chopped onion (with some garlic perhaps) in a little oil, add half a glass of wine if you have some open, and when the onion is soft tip in the contents of the tin. Add any suitable flavouring – fennel seed for fish, rosemary for chicken, etc., and season to taste. When the mixture is really hot add the meat or fish, cut or divided into pieces, and transfer to a casserole. If you have some yogurt (I try never to be without it) spread a ½-inch-thick layer over the top. Sprinkle with paprika or sesame seeds and put in a really hot oven for 10 minutes. The quick accompaniment to this is rice, and perhaps some frozen peas or beans.

Cooking time: if you start with the rice, 20 minutes flat, or 15 if you're nippy.

HUGH JOHNSON

STARTER

Orange Elevator is a much prettier and more interesting drink than Buck's Fizz. Instead of using orange juice, you scrape minute pieces of the aromatic zest off the surface of a handsome orange. You pour a glass of Champagne (or sparkling wine), and you sprinkle a good pinch of the zest in the glass. It sinks, but the rising bubbles bring it back to the surface, whence it sinks again, the whole thing resembling the elevators in Hyatt hotels. The better the Champagne, the more it costs; but it's fun with El Cheapo too.

ENTRÉES

Explore. The following wine regions make *much* better wine than you think. Australia, Bairrada, Catalonia, Chile, Corbières, Corsica, Friuli-Venezia Giulia, New Zealand, Trentino-Alto-Adige – and the Isle of Wight!

AFTERS

For a clear head: cool claret. Clairette de Die (like a French Asti Spumante) for cerebration. Cointreau on the rocks for celebration. Hocks for the box.

My surrealistic drawing depicts myself at the top of the trifle looking at my bowl of pasta, because I feel that food should look very imaginative and should be a talking point amongst the guests.

To close the meal I always serve tea instead of coffee because it is very cleansing to the palate. I like to use a mixture of teas. If you don't go to America a lot and can't use the ones like the brand of pink tea made with cherrybark and hibiscus flowers and peppermint called Red Zinger, then use jasmine tea with maybe a bit of spearmint tea mixed with it.

For a large pot you need about 1 heaped tablespoon tea, 1 tablespoon sugar, a chopped-up orange, chopped lemon, almond essence and maybe a few mint leaves if they are around. This makes a clear refreshing tea that is always a talking point of the evening. The large pot I am talking about makes enough tea to fill about 20 small coffee cups.

Zandra Rhodes
Party
menu

Fettucini alla crema alla Zandra Rhodes
Zandra Rhodes Trifle
Tea à la maison

2 handfuls pasta per person

A selection of sliced or chopped vegetables, anything green and lovely, e.g. asparagus (if in season and economical), Brussels sprouts (cleaned and halved or quartered), spring greens, courgettes, green peppers, etc. I also use onions and cauliflower florets

4 oz butter, plus a little extra

Salt

Peppercorns

2 tablespoons chopped sage

2 cups double cream

1 cup grated cheese, preferably Emmental or Gruyère

I have a large Chinese steamer, but a steamer over a saucepan would do. I put salted water on to boil underneath my steamer and when it boils I put in the pasta and cook it for 5 minutes. I then put the vegetables that will take longest to cook into the steamer and cook them for 5 minutes. By now the pasta should be ready, so I strain it and add the quick-cooking vegetables, such as asparagus, green peppers and courgettes, to the steamer. I then continue cooking the vegetables for about 3 minutes, while I prepare the pasta.

I put the cooked pasta in a large, warmed bowl with 4 oz butter, salt and freshly ground pepper. I do not use a grinder for the pepper which I regard as the main essential flavour of the dish; instead, I use a pestle and mortar and grind the peppercorns coarsely, so it is like adding gravel to the food. I then throw in the sage, cream and grated cheese and mix thoroughly, tasting to see if there is enough salt. If I have any other fresh herbs, such as parsley, I add them as well as they give the dish a really wonderful flavour.

Next, I remove the vegetables from the steamer and add them to the pasta with a little more butter, then I mix the whole lot together and serve immediately.

This classic party trifle is best made the night before because you have to leave the jelly to set.

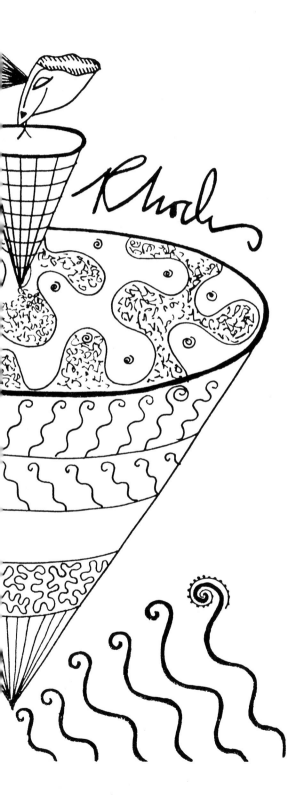

Swiss roll or sponge cake, sliced
1 large tin mixed fruit
2 Chivers jellies (I like the look of the green ones best)
1 tin Carnation milk, topped up with ordinary milk to make 1 pint
1 pint milk
5 heaped tablespoons Bird's custard powder
4 rounded tablespoons sugar
Almond essence
Double cream
Vanilla essence

Arrange the Swiss roll and the strained fruit in a glass bowl. Use the fruit juice and water to make up the jelly, pour it over the cake and fruit and leave it to set.

The custard, which should be thick and smooth, should also be made in advance. Heat the milk, then put the sugar and custard powder in a bowl and gradually add the milk and a few drops of almond essence, stirring constantly. Stir the custard occasionally while it is cooling to prevent a skin from forming, then set aside.

Next day, put the custard on top of the jelly in the bowl, then add a layer of whipped double cream flavoured with sugar and vanilla essence. Patterns can then be applied with cherries, angelica and hundreds and thousands.

WEIGHT

One Imperial pound (lb) = 454 grams (g)

Imperial	Approx. metric equivalent
1 oz	25g
2 oz	50g
3 oz	75g
4 oz	100-125g
5 oz	150g
6 oz	175g
7 oz	200g
8 oz	225g
9 oz	250g
10 oz	275g
11 oz	300g
12 oz	325-350g
13 oz	375g
14 oz	400g
15 oz	425g
16 oz (1 lb)	450g
1½ lb	700g
2 lb	900g
2½ lb	1.1kg
3 lb	1.4kg
3½ lb	1.6kg
4 lb	1.8kg
4½ lb	2kg

LIQUID CAPACITY

One Imperial pint (20 fluid oz) = 569 millilitres (ml)

Imperial	Approx. metric equivalent
1 fluid oz	25ml
2 fluid oz	50ml
3 fluid oz	75ml
4 fluid oz	100-125ml
5 fluid oz (¼ pint)	150ml
6 fluid oz	175ml
7 fluid oz	200ml
8 fluid oz	225ml
9 fluid oz	250ml
10 fluid oz (½ pint)	275-300ml
15 fluid oz (¾ pint)	425ml
20 fluid oz (1 pint)	570-600ml
1¼ pints	700ml
1½ pints	900ml
2 pints	1.2 litres
2½ pints	1.5 litres
3 pints	1.7 litres

OVEN TEMPERATURES

Gas mark	°F	°C
½	250	130
1	275	140
2	300	150
3	325	170
4	350	180
5	375	190
6	400	200
7	425	220
8	450	230
9	475	240

AN IMPERIAL/AMERICAN GUIDE TO SOLID AND LIQUID MEASURES

SOLID MEASURES

Imperial	American
1 lb butter or margarine	2 cups
1 lb flour	4 cups
1 lb granulated or castor sugar	2 cups
1 lb icing sugar	3 cups
8 oz rice	1 cup

LIQUID MEASURES

1 Imperial pint = 20 fluid oz
1 American pint = 16 fluid oz

Imperial	American
¼ pint liquid	⅔ cup liquid*
½ pint	1¼ cups
¾ pint	2 cups
1 pint	2½ cups
1½ pints	3¾ cups
2 pints	5 cups

CONTRIBUTORS AND ARTISTS

Maxime Adam-Tessier, French sculptor, benefactor to Dept. of Sculpture (pp73, 80); Kenneth Armitage Hon. Dr RCA, Visiting Lecturer in Sculpture (p100); Sue Balfre (p47); Gregg Becker (pp72, 145); Lutz Becker, ex-Tutor of Film (p94); John Bellany, former student (pp62-3); Jeny Bennett, Secretary in Administration (p45); Gerald Benney, ex-Professor of Silversmithing and Jewelry (p127); Quentin Blake, Senior Tutor of Illustration (pp43, 66, 99); Gill Bradley (pp61, 142); John Bradley (p50); John Bratby RA, painter (p103); Louise Brierley (p29); Krysia Brochocka, former student (pp11, 33, 109); Joanne Brogden, Professor of Fashion Design (pp57, 58, 76); Peter Brookes, (p48); Robert Buhler RA, ex-Tutor of Painting (pp14-15, 120); Emma Calder (p126); Mel Calman, Visiting Lecturer in Illustration (p137); Margaret Calvert, Tutor of Graphics (p19); Cameron A. Campbell (p82); Sir Hugh Casson CH KCVO PPRA, ex-Provost, ex-Professor of Architecture (pp71, 125, 154); Lady (Margaret) Casson, ex-Tutor of Interior Design (pp21, 71, 125, 154); Joan Catlin, ex-Assistant Registrar (pp90, 126, 145, 148); Richard Cawley, former student of Fashion (pp22, 31); Emma Chichester-Clark, former student of Illustration (pp53, 77); Alan Couldridge, Tutor of Fashion, and Valerie Couldridge, ex-Tutor of Fashion (p64); Paul Cox, former student of Illustration (p102); Theo Crosby ARA RIBA FSIAD, Member of Council, Pentagram (p122); Per Dahlberg, former student of Illustration and Audio Visual (p92); Andrew Davidson, former student of Illustration (p69); Ed Day, former student (p130); Cherry Denman (p11, 101); Shaun Dew (p28); Lilian Dodd, Technician in Textiles (p32); Fred Dubery, Senior Tutor of Photography (pp26-7, 87); Alf Dunn, Tutor of Printmaking (p55, 104); Lucy Dupre (p133); Dan Fern, Head of Illustration Department (p59); Monica Fine (p42); Hannah Firmin, former student of Illustration (pp70, 114, 146); Alan Fletcher, Graphic Designer, Pentagram (p134); Michael Foreman, Visiting Lecturer in Illustration (p129); Julia Foskett, former student; Peter de Francia, ex-Professor of Painting (pp78, 152); Christopher Frayling, Professor of Cultural

History (p143); Terry Frost, former student (p147); Reg Gadney, ex-Pro-Rector, ex-Tutor of Film (p123); David Gentleman, book illustrator, Honorary Fellow of the College (p115); Jane Gibson (p48); Bobby Gill, Tutor of Graphics (p54, 107); Dr Giorgio Giugiaro Hon. Dr RCA (p40); Dominic de Grunne, ex-Tutor of Cultural History (pp70, 72); John Golding, ex-Senior Tutor of Painting (p38); Dr Robert Goodden CBE RDI RIBA, ex-Pro-Rector and ex-Professor of Silversmithing and Jewelry (pp61, 146); James Gowan FRIBA, Tutor of Architecture and Design Studies (p113); Carolyn Gowdy (p90); Alistair Grant, Professor of Printmaking (p118-19); Frank Guille, Head of Furniture Department (p153); Richard Guyatt, ex-Rector, ex-Professor of Graphic Design (p144); Donald Hamilton Fraser RA, ex-Tutor of Painting, and Judy Hamilton Fraser (p108); Nicholas Hardcastle (p132); John Hedgecoe, Pro-Rector, Professor of Photography (p52); Julia Hedgecoe, friend of RCA (pp20, 52, 95); Michael Heindorff, Tutor of Painting (p18); Sue Hilton (p68); Susan Hilton (p88); Paul Hogarth, ex-Tutor and Visiting Lecturer in Illustration (p34); Sarah Holland (p96); the late Lord Howard, former College Treasurer, Member of Council (p99); Paul Huxley, Professor of Painting (p151); Kenneth Ireland, Industrial Design Technician (p129); Kristin Jacob (p12, 45, 117); Hugh Johnson, friend of RCA (p155); Leslie Johnson (p152); Aziz R. Khan, Steward, Queen's Gate (p68); Phillip King, Professor of Sculpture (p44); Mak Kum Siew, former student (p86); Peter Latham Smith (p84); Joy Law, ex-Exhibitions Officer (also Jenny Law and Katie Law) (pp47, 53, 77, 88, 101, 142, 150) and Nicholas Law (p42); Joanna Lewis (p13); Robin Levien, former student (p102); Valerie Lyons, Student Admissions Clerk (p85, 114); Ann Marshall (p148); Derek Martin (p10); Gary McCarver (p112, 150); Bernard Meadows, ex-Professor of Sculpture (p18); Sir Yehudi Menuhin, Senior Fellow of the College (p97); Anne Morley, ex-Secretary of Cultural History (p133); Bernard Myers, Corresponding Professor of RCA (pp46, 111); the late Henry Moore, former student, ex-Head of Sculpture, First

Honorary Doctor of RCA (p89); Mechthild Nawiasky, ex-Tutor of Cultural History (p24, 28); Bernard Nevill, Professor of Textiles (p117); the late Roger Nicholson, ex-Professor of Textiles (pp16, 41, 136); Cathy Noble (p109); Siobhan Noonan (p140); John Norris Wood, Tutor of Illustration (pp128, 138-9); the late Peter O'Malley, ex-Tutor of Ceramics (p116); Sir Duncan Oppenheim, ex-Chairman of Council (pp17, 75); Chris Orr, Tutor of Engraving (p74); Professor Eduardo Paolozzi, Tutor of Ceramics and Glass (p36-7); James Park, Head of Textile Design (p135); Gillian Patterson, Tutor of Painting (p29); Simon Phillips (p100); John Piper CH, painter, and Myfanwy Piper (p98); Patrick Procktor, Visiting Tutor of Printmaking (p110); Lord Queensberry, ex-Professor of Ceramics and Glass (p20, 95); Zandra Rhodes Hon. Dr RCA, former student of Textiles (pp156-57); Sheila Robinson, Tutor of Illustration (p149); Marta Rogoyska, ex-Visiting Lecturer in Textiles (p92); Leonard Rosoman OBE RA, ex-Tutor of Painting, visiting Tutor of Illustration (p106); Michael Rothenstein RA, printmaker (p30); Sue Scullard (p81); Charles Shearer, former student of Illustration (p32); Christine Simpson (p56, 85); Brian Smith, ex-Professor of Design Management (p124); Jean Southwood, ex-Catering Officer (pp12, 16, 82, 137); Ruskin Spear RA, ex-Tutor of Painting (p91); Herbert Spencer, ex-Professor of Graphics (p49); Lady Spender, ex-Tutor of Cultural History (p112); Michael Starling, ex-Tutor of Industrial Design (p50); Jocelyn Stevens, Rector (p130); Brian Tattersfield, Visiting Lecturer in Graphic Design (p23); Blaise Thompson (pp97, 121); Julian Trevelyan Hon. Fellow RCA, former Tutor of Printmaking (p39); Anne Tyrrell, Tutor of Fashion Design (p65); Floris van den Broecke, Professor of Furniture (p83); Dosia Verney, ex-Council Member (p84, 132); Sybil Waldock, ex-Secretary, Registry (pp69, 81, 96, 121); Hilary Watson, former student of Cultural History (p140); Carel Weight CBE RA, Emeritus Professor of Painting (p60); Jessica Widden, ex-Student Admissions Clerk (p10); Virginia Wilkinson (p33); Rosemary Wilson, Rector's Secretary (p13, 56).

Recipe on page 60 reproduced by kind permission of Elisabeth Ayrton from *English Provincial Cooking* (Mitchell Beazley).